A YEAR IN PARIS

A YEAR IN PARIS

Season by Season in the
City of Light

John Baxter

HARPER PERENNIAL

NEW YORK • LONDON • TORONTO • SYDNEY • NEW DELHI • AUCKLAND

HARPER ● PERENNIAL

HarperCollins books may be purchased for educational, business, or
sales promotional use. For information please email the Special Markets Department at SPsales@harpercollins.com.

FIRST EDITION

Designed by Jamie Kerner and Jen Overstreet

Library of Congress Cataloging-in-Publication Data has been applied
for.

ISBN 978-0-06-284688-4 (PBK.)

19 20 21 22 23   LSC   10 9 8 7 6 5 4 3 2 1

Paris in the snow, 1879.

To Marie-Dominique and Louise,
around whom my world turns.

Between the Swiss snows and the icy winter fogs of Germany on the one side, and the mists and rain and perpetual dampness of England on the other, her cool mild sky shot with veiled sunlight overhung a land of temperate beauty and temperate wealth. Farther north, man might grow austere or gross, farther south idle and improvident: France offered the happy mean which the poets are forever celebrating, and the French were early aware that the poets were right.

—Edith Wharton, *French Ways and Their Meaning*

Contents

INTRODUCTION:
HARVEST OF DREAMS

*Paris 8me. Sunday, June 1990. 18°C. Blue skies, and towers
of white cumulus, looking as solid as cauliflowers, boiling up
toward the jet stream. A light breeze carries the native odors of a
city, black coffee, unfiltered tobacco, gasoline.*

Sometimes it simply happens. You just *know*. So I can remember to the day when I first learned of the love affair between Paris and the seasons.

I was, I suppose, in a state of hypersensitivity, attuned to the subtlest of signals. Just a year before I had been happily settled in Los Angeles, living at last in the city I'd selected as my spiritual home after reading the novels of Raymond Chandler in adolescence and seeing the films of Billy Wilder. The years in Europe and my native Australia were like old snapshots, colors faded by the Californian sun. That past and those people no longer existed. I woke each morning to a perpetual present in the city acknowledged as the capital of Now.

My fantasy survived a little more than a year. Then a woman reappeared from that past, and overnight I just *knew*—that imperative again—that in defiance of all logic I had to follow her to France, of whose language I spoke barely a word and where I knew no one but her.

Seven months had passed, and I still moved around Paris with the caution of an earthquake survivor, hand never far from a railing, not sure the ground wouldn't once again open beneath my feet.

A friend had phoned that Sunday morning in June 1990 to babble, "You *must* take a look at the Champs-Élysées today. You won't believe it!"

The more I pressed him about what I'd see, the more evasive he became. "I don't want to ruin it. Just . . . *go!*"

So as an escalator at the Franklin D. Roosevelt metro station carried me up to street level, I still had no idea what to expect.

Emerging into the sunlight, I looked up the hill toward the Arc de Triomphe . . . and found that my friend was right. I didn't believe it.

Overnight, one of the widest and busiest avenues in Paris had become a field of wheat. Grain, waist-high, filled the street to the Arc de Triomphe at the top of the hill.

On both sides of the avenue the pavement was clear, and cross streets had been kept open for emergency vehicles. In a few small enclosures scattered around the edges, people demonstrated country crafts: basket weaving, sheep shearing. Otherwise, there was just wheat.

Steel barriers enclosed the field. I grabbed one and, resisting the pull of the crowd pouring up behind me from the metro, hung on as

The Champs-Élysées under wheat, 1990.

I took in the sight. A man in a shapeless smock, a straw hat, and bare feet came out of a cross street, leading a cart pulled by two oxen. He was chewing a stalk of wheat and appeared unconcerned at blocking a thoroughfare where on a normal day it was almost a capital offense to pause, let alone park.

I stayed there for the rest of the afternoon, caught in an eddy of time that returned Paris 1990 to an era three centuries in the past, when no laws applied except those of the seasons. The Arc de Triomphe dominated the hilltop, celebrating the victories of Napoléon Bonaparte, but this was no day for emperors. The wheat, bowing lazily in the breeze, put worldly pomp in its place. One saw why Katharine Lee Bates, who wrote the lyrics of "America the Beautiful," specified "amber waves of grain" as an element of the new nation. No wonder the presidential hopes of Michael Dukakis never recovered from his 1989 suggestion to Iowa's corn farmers that they replant with such boutique vegetables as Belgian endive. Fields of grain were the irreducible minimum of a civilization, the rock on which it stood.

Implicit in the presence of this field here today in the heart of Paris was the message that France, with the same population as Britain but three times the area, belonged to those who controlled the land. Defy them, as Louis XVI had done in 1789, and you risked being handed your head.

At that time of year, the setting sun lingers for a few minutes in the very center of the Arc de Triomphe, sending a blaze of light the length of the Champs-Élysées. As it did so, engines growled on the other side of the arch. A minute later, a line of combine harvesters belching smoke lumbered into sight and crawled toward us, devouring the wheat.

In their wake rose a golden cloud of dust from which materialized hundreds of young men and women, each carrying a spear shaped like a wheat stalk. From the watchers rose a collective sigh of satisfaction and awe.

That night's television news explained that the day had been a demonstration by 1,500 farmers on behalf of French agriculture. Three thousand six hundred tons of wheat, grown to maturity around Paris on pallets, were trucked in overnight to stun us three hundred thousand who came to gawk.

Politics had provided the pretext, but one sensed that the farmers would have staged this show just for the pleasure of it. They had gone into the streets often in the past, sometimes to celebrate but more often, as in this case, to warn. The beliefs behind such manifestations were already ancient when Christianity came squalling into the world. Between France, the land, and the seasons, it was a matter of blood.

A WINTER'S TALE

Richebourg, Île-de-France. December 1990. 1 degree below zero C. Hailstones rattle like gravel against double layers of glass. Beyond, in a gray murk of near-horizontal freezing rain, ancient trees, trunks sodden and black, lurk like gallows.

Had the weather been this bad in Bethlehem, Jesus would have imitated the ancient gods and waited until spring to be born.

Six months later, I tried to recapture a sense of that day: the glare; the grain's dry, vegetal smell; the sting of the sun through my thin jacket. It was hopeless. However warm the memory, the chill of December quenched it.

For almost a week storms had battered the sixteenth-century house in Richebourg, one hundred kilometers from Paris, where we were spending the holidays.

The house, my mother-in-law's country home, was an unexpected dividend of marrying into an old French family. Hand-hewn chestnut beams, already old when Bonaparte became emperor, supported this onetime farmhouse that in its indestructibility could have served as a metaphor for France's landowners, the backbone of the nation.

The church and the aristocracy, known as the First and Second Estates, barely survived the revolution of 1789, but if that bloody conflict had a winner, it was the Third Estate: the landowners, farmers, and people in business

As unrest bubbled in January 1789, Abbé Sieyès, the most perceptive and charismatic of spokesmen for the disenfranchised, warned of the cost should this segment of the population, the nation's most numerous, be further ignored. "What is the Third Estate?" he demanded rhetorically. "Everything. What has it been until now in the political order? Nothing. What does it want to be? Something." Within five years the king and his family were dead, along with most of the privileged classes.

Since then, the influence of primary producers has grown. To a degree greater in France than in any other country, rural life, its products and manifestations, and the effects of nature and the seasons influence thought, language, literature, religion, art, and politics.

Warm and dry behind a meter of stone as the storm raged, I couldn't help feeling smug. Somewhere out there our neighbors were celebrating France's best-loved feast, but they might as well have been on the moon.

The table was cleared of the debris from the lunch for twenty that my wife, Marie-Dominique, our daughter, Louise, and I had, in what had become a tradition, prepared and served. (Foie gras, guinea fowl capon, *gratin dauphinois*, haricots verts, pavlova *maison*.) In this hierarchical society I was technically the chef, a duty I'd accepted almost as soon as I arrived in France—my passport into a family of painters, academics, and authors, none of whom could boil water without a recipe.

Meal over, older guests had reconvened at the other end of the house to gossip with my aunt-in-law Françoise, who, as the village mayor, stood guard over decades of scandal. A creak from overhead signaled where a couple of younger cousins had sneaked off for some stolen sex in one of the tiny bedrooms wedged under the eaves, where the beds, carpentered from local timber early in the nineteenth century and topped with sheets of linen and quilts stuffed with goose feathers, were drenched in generations of erotic history.

But what had become of our friend Paul, the sole Englishman at the table? The lunch had been his introduction to the French holiday. He'd appeared to take it in his stride, chatting with his neighbors on either side and accepting without obvious disappointment the absence of a Christmas pudding.

I hadn't seen him since he helped clear away the dishes. If he had any sense, he was probably, like me, getting ready for a postprandial snooze.

Settling deeper into the chair, I eased off my shoes and closed my eyes . . .

Paul appeared in the doorway. Rubbing his hands together, he peered through the window into the sleet and freezing mist.

"Looks like it's clearing up," he said. "Fancy a stroll?"

WHAT *IS* IT ABOUT FRANCE?

Rue Férou, Paris 6me. July 1927. 1 a.m. Dizzy from three bottles of wine shared with Archibald MacLeish, Ernest Hemingway, unused to modern plumbing, yanks what he believes to be the lavatory flush in his new apartment and instead pulls a skylight down on his head. Waiting to be sewn up at the American Hospital of Paris in Neuilly, he's reminded by the pain, blood, and chloroform of being blown up on the Italian front in 1918. The idea of a novel based on those experiences forms in his head; call it A Farewell to Arms.

As of 2017, the world's top ten preferred tourist destinations, in order of popularity, were France, the United States, Spain, China, Italy, the United Kingdom, Germany, Mexico, Thailand, and Malaysia.

Anything seem odd about this list?

Most people traveling to Spain, Italy, Mexico, Thailand, and Malaysia cite "climate" as an attraction. All are warm countries.

Many visitors to the United States likewise head for Florida, California, and Nevada—sunshine states.

And yet France, not notably sunny nor rich in tourist resorts and, moreover, hampered by a difficult language and a population not always welcoming to foreigners, tops the list, and has done so consistently for decades.

What *is* it about France?

The words change, but the question people ask is always the same: Why do we idealize France above so many other countries?

Not that the others don't have their champions. A villa in Tuscany figures in the fantasies of many. For others, it's the sun of Greece or Spain. A smaller percentage seeks the asceticism of Scandinavia or the sprawl of Russia and China. Some even raise their voices in favor of Australia.

As for cities, it would be a dull stick who was not drawn to Rome's antiquities, the seething energy of Beijing and Tokyo, culturally rich New York and Berlin, the pageantry of Madrid, the grace of Saint Petersburg, and what Jorge Luis Borges called the "splintered labyrinth" of London.

But no capital excites the passions like Paris. Berlin, far from being a moveable feast, remains stubbornly immobile. No woman speaks with longing of "a Brussels dress," nor do we, in search of culinary excellence, head for Zurich. And not even the most bittersweet reminiscence of Prague or Lisbon or Athens conveys the poignancy of "I remember . . . once . . . in Paris . . ."

So I ask again: What *is* it about France?

Truthfully, we who live here can no more understand our fidelity than we can analyze the attraction of a loved one. The question belongs with that other exasperated query, "What do you *see* in him?"

I had plenty of time to ponder this question as I suited up that Christmas Day for my walk with Paul. Only when I'd wrapped myself in enough heavy clothing for a trip on a deep-sea trawler did I dare step outside and guide him down the village's main street.

We were, not surprisingly, entirely alone. Even the dogs that on a normal day would have signaled our passing with a barrage of barks and snarls had the sense to remain indoors. Before Pieter Brueghel in the sixteenth century, European artists shunned winter, painting only green fields and sunny skies. One could see why. December was not a month of which anybody would wish to be reminded.

I led Paul around the highlights of Richebourg, such as they were: Its sole shop, shuttered and derelict since supermarkets opened in nearby towns. The marketplace next door, once the site of busy trade on weekends with farmers selling their produce, now used as overflow parking for the village's biggest employer, a hospital for brain-damage cases. Many of them were survivors of accidents on France's widely admired freeways, like the one a kilometer away, whose traffic was audible on quieter nights.

Rural decline was nothing new. Richebourg had been going downhill since the Middle Ages. Farmworkers weren't the only people forced off the land by mechanization. The thirteenth-century church where Louise had been christened was, as usual, bolted shut. With religion at a low ebb, mass was celebrated here only one Sunday in four, the same priest serving three other dioceses in rotation. For the christening, we'd had to hire a priest from a pool of the unemployed. He arrived with his own vestments, like a bit-part actor who supplies his own tuxedo. Have Faith, Will Travel.

A narrow lane between rough stone walls led to the village's communal laundry. The oblong pond, fed by a spring and edged in granite slabs, where generations of women had knelt to pound their washing, looked almost quaint, though the thought of immersing my hands in that gray water was enough to freeze my blood.

Yet Paul, even as we trudged into a wind loaded with stinging fragments of ice, seemed to be enjoying himself.

There was a Viking strain in the British character that drew them to harsh places: T. E. Lawrence to Arabia, Robert Falcon Scott to Antarctica, George Mallory to Everest. Before Mallory left for the ascent from which he never returned, someone asked why he was risking his life to climb a mountain. One can imagine the pitying look with which he gave his famous response: "Because it's *there*."

The British are, after all, the only nation with a Christmas carol that actually celebrates the cold. Who else would sing words like this?

In the bleak midwinter, frosty wind made moan,
Earth stood hard as iron, water like a stone;

Snow had fallen, snow on snow, snow on snow,
In the bleak midwinter, long ago.

I'd heard Paul argue that fresh air ventilated the sinuses and cleansed the lungs. In this spirit, whole generations of Britons had endured cold showers and plunged into ponds from which the ice had barely been chipped. As a boy, travel writer Eric Newby was taught to sniff some saltwater every morning. "As a result," he wrote in his memoir *Something Wholesale: My Life and Times in the Rag Trade*, "I contracted sinusitis, and was told by a specialist I consulted that this was an outmoded exercise that led to acute inflammation of the nasal cavities." Ronald Reagan articulated the American view of such practices. Of his presidential opponent Jimmy Carter he said, "A man who says he enjoys a cold shower every morning will lie about other things."

Paul and I each represented a national response to the weather. Britons defied it. Australians like me—and Americans, come to that—ignored it until some hurricane or flood or bushfire overwhelmed them. And the French?

Contradicting Mark Twain, who, among many others, said that everybody talks about the weather but nobody does anything about it, the French embraced it.

Assessing how it might be most agreeably enjoyed, or at least endured, they created rituals to extract the maximum satisfaction from the climate and its seasonal variations. Weather was woven into the culture in a manner that made even minute variations a pretext for reflection, celebration, and delight.

Once, driven by ambition and misplaced patriotism, some men even tried to redesign the year to fit France's idea of the seasons. How that came about, what grandiose individuals were behind it, and what became of them and their project says a lot about the nation where I'd decided to make my home.

3

DOG DAYS

Paris 16me. August 1976. 26°C. Dust as fine as talcum sifts through shutters closed against the sun. It films the black lacquer of the Bechstein grand, makes even more slick the waxed wooden blocks of the parquet floor, coats the cream-and-green enamel of the kitchen's antique refrigerator and stove, grits between the teeth in the aftermath of a kiss.

FIRST HEARD OF THE REPUBLICAN CALENDAR IN THE 1970S, WHEN I lived in London. The year is irrelevant, but men were wearing their hair long, women theirs short. Flowered shirts and beads were the rage, and everyone seemed to be playing Elton John's "Don't Let the Sun Go Down on Me."

Céline and I hooked up at a party in Chelsea, London's equivalent of Greenwich Village, Trastevere, Montparnasse. The hostess was her daughter, Kissy, a bosomy twentysomething with pretensions to art. But her real talent lay in having her cake and eating it, a skill she'd exploited to score a show at one of the pop-up galleries that sprouted around East London like mushrooms after rain and expired just as speedily.

Her apartment showed more flair than her canvases. In a style best described as "Moorish whorehouse," she'd draped filmy fabric from the ceilings, turning every room into a tent under which incense blended with cannabis smoke in an exotic miasma.

Céline, slim and pale with short dark hair, belonged to that segment of women diplomatically described by the French as *femmes d'un certain âge*. Her black silk trouser suit sometimes masked the shape of her body, at other times clung to it, evidence for the suggestion that silk was invented in order that women could go naked while still clothed. What won me, however, was her voice. If French is the language of diplomacy, English spoken with a French accent must be the language of seduction.

A friend once confided to me a preference for "older women with a Past." I responded with a line spoken by Brigitte Auber in Alfred Hitchcock's *To Catch a Thief*, in which she plays a hot young Frenchwoman. Mocking Cary Grant's preference for Grace Kelly over her, she asks, "Why buy an old car if you can get a new one cheaper? It will run better and last longer."

If I had ever harbored such prejudices against age, Céline demolished them. So this was why Charles Swann in Marcel Proust's *À la recherche du temps perdu* (*In Search of Lost Time*) could moan of his attraction to Odette de Crécy, "To think that I wasted years of my life, that I wanted to die, that I felt my deepest love, for a woman who did not appeal to me, who was not my type!"

Some relationships fly in air so thin that any conventional attraction would fall of its own weight. Ours justified the use of words like "enchantment." After the party, we walked back in silence through the empty streets and climbed the six floors to my apartment.

"So bare," she said, looking around my living room. "No pictures?"

Bare? I'd aimed for minimalist.

She strolled into the bedroom and shrugged off her jacket. A slither of silk.

"You do not like a big bed?"

Queen-size had always seemed large enough, but now I wondered.

She began to undress. Lingerie to *die* for. Coffee silk, with lace along the hems.

"You have candles? No?"

She draped her scarf over the lamp. What I'd taken for black was deep purple. Shadows took on the soft bloom of a bruise.

Our affair ignited that night. Once she went home, I slipped across to Paris every few weeks to spend a weekend in her sprawling apartment in the *seizième*.

Kissy kept a room there but never visited, at least not when I was around, and though a *femme de ménage* came twice a week to clean, all I ever saw of her was a fresh wax shine on the parquet and new linen on the bed. Woven so densely it felt heavy, as though soaked in water, each sheet was embroidered with an incomprehensible monogram, signifying Céline's marriage to a husband even less evident than Kissy, barely more than a phantom presence somewhere on the far side of the world.

Years later, I saw my experience with Céline mirrored in *Le*

Divorce, a novel by the American writer Diane Johnson. Her main character is an American woman who takes a much older Frenchman as a lover. Reveling in the way he instructs her in the intricacies of life in Paris, she muses, "If you didn't know where to look, you could pass your whole life with no sense of what you were missing." As far as France was concerned, Céline was as much teacher as lover.

That was when I first heard of Philippe-François-Nazaire Fabre d'Églantine—"Fabre of the Wild Rose"—and his plan to redesign the year, cutting and shaping the seasons as a couturier tailors a gown to show off the best points of his client.

It was August, a month that descends on Paris like a curse. Empty streets echo with the clatter of jackhammers as café owners rush through renovations before their clientele floods back in early September. By noon it was too hot to move, to eat, certainly to make love, so we read and dozed, pressing to our foreheads the glasses of homemade limeade, beaded with moisture, that we drank by the liter.

In another room a radio was tuned almost inaudibly to a jazz station. After a few bars of one tune, Céline opened her violet eyes and murmured a few words:

"Balayé par septembre, notre amour d'un été . . ."

They meant nothing to me, but I thought I recognized the singer's husky baritone.

"Is that Aznavour?"

"Yes. *'Paris au mois d'août.'* 'Paris in the Month of August.'"

At the time, I caught only the sense of the song. Later I looked up the words, and their translation.

Swept away by September
Our summertime love
Sadly comes apart
And dies, in the past tense.
Even though I expected it,
My heart empties itself of everything.
It could even be mistaken
For Paris in the month of August.

The words caught the lassitude of what the French call *le ca-nicule*, so much more evocative than our "heat wave." *Canicule* because these are the "dog days," when Sirius, the Dog Star, is in the ascendant. The languorous despair evoked by the song was almost pleasurable. As Noël Coward said, "Extraordinary how potent cheap music is."

"*Comme il est triste*," Céline sighed as she listened. "Just right for Thermidor."

"Thermidor?" I said. "Like lobster thermidor?"

She punched my arm, but playfully. "No! Not like the lobster—or not *only* like the lobster, at least. Why is it always food with you? Or films."

"Tell me, then."

She let her book fall and leaned back on the cushions of the couch.

"Very well. But first you must kiss me."

Breathlessly, I obeyed her.

Distributing hats for horses during a Paris heat wave, 1890s.

4

ON AN ISLAND IN THE SEINE

Place Dauphine, Paris 6me. July 2002. 9 a.m. 29°C.
Fine red dust blankets the city. Settling overnight, the
coppery powder films windscreens and dulls the hue of
flowers. In sidewalk cafés people rub their fingertips
together, sniff them like a spice, and nod as if in ap-
preciation. No need to mention the Sahara; it is in
their eyes.

IT WAS MORE THAN TEN YEARS BEFORE I MOVED PERMANENTLY TO
Paris. The identity of my companion changed, but Paris remained
much the same.

Born on the world's largest island, I struggled to adjust to life on
one of the smallest.

The Île de la Cité, a sliver of land in the middle of the river
Seine, would have made a roomy but not ostentatiously large Australian backyard. But differences in size were dwarfed by the cultural abyss between my old life and the new. Speaking little French
and knowing not a soul in France, I had nevertheless followed a
woman halfway across the world to share her tiny studio within

The Île de la Cité.

sight of the Louvre. No Robinson Crusoe was ever more comprehensively marooned.

And yet I'd seldom been happier—a bliss that only increased when a few months later, Marie-Dominique became pregnant. Occasionally, a fragment of verse from Dylan Thomas's poem "Fern Hill" drifted through my mind: "I sang in my chains like the sea."

If one had to be beached in France, there were worse places than the Île de la Cité. Imagine an ocean liner of stone, moored in the very heart of Paris. Its prow points north, toward where, almost two hundred kilometers away, the Seine joins the English Channel at Le

Havre. Dominating the stern of this vessel is the cathedral of Notre Dame, the bells of which—Quasimodo's bells!—toll over the city each Sunday.

Clustered at the other end are the Sainte-Chapelle, with its soaring Gothic arches and stained glass; the Conciergerie, where Louis XVI and his family languished before their execution; and France's high court, the Palais de Justice. And beyond these, at the very bow of this vessel, is Place Dauphine.

Triangular and no larger than a couple of tennis courts, this had once been the kitchen garden of what is now the Palais de Justice. None of that vegetation remained. The surface, like that of many public places in Paris, was coarse beige grit, hard packed. And though there were trees—about twenty chestnuts—they existed only on sufferance. Every few years they disappeared, unplugged like so many light bulbs, to be replaced with saplings that by the summer had come into leaf and provided a fresh canopy of shade. It was my introduction to the variety of Paris and a culture that, like an art gallery, periodically closed, to reemerge displaying new images, insights, and experiences.

From the moment Henry IV laid it out in the 1600s, Place Dauphine was a select address, and a magnet for celebrities. Four centuries had not changed that. Most days, portly stage actor and occasional film star Jean Desailly walked his Saint Bernard here. Standing by in approval, he'd watch as this massive pooch, with the casual condescension of someone signing an autograph, deposited a turd the size of a torpedo. Movie actor and singer Yves Montand, another neighbor, gave interviews on a bench just below our window. Later, we inherited his housekeeper. I'm still enough of a fan to be pleased that my shirts were ironed with the expertise once lavished on a man who'd slept with both Édith Piaf and Marilyn Monroe.

In 1928, André Breton, founder of surrealism, conferred immortality on Place Dauphine by using it in his novel *Nadja* as the home of its mysterious eponymous heroine. Calling it "one of the most profoundly secluded places I know of," he continued, "I confess that this place frightens me," but he overcame his disquiet to further observe that the three-cornered space deserved its description as "the pubic triangle of Paris."

It's in the nature of pubic triangles to be discreet. Every pedestrian crossing the Pont Neuf passed the narrow lane that gives access, but few turned aside to enter. A seventeenth-century hauteur in its buildings discouraged loitering. Even dogs attempting to irrigate the trees were defeated by the metal grilles that enclosed them. Finding no soft spot in the gritty sand, they made a desultory swipe or two with their back feet and got the hell out.

In *Nadja*, Breton implied that his heroine knew of other mysteries in Place Dauphine, even beyond those that were visible. "She is certain that an underground tunnel passes under our feet," he wrote, "[and] is disturbed by the thought of what has already occurred in this square and will occur here in the future."

Like many of his pronouncements, this was prescient. Just after I arrived, the city excavated a vast pit under the square to construct a subterranean parking lot. Sand, trees, benches, and streetlamps were then put back in place, leaving, aside from a discreet pedestrian entrance, barely a sign of the garage's existence. Nadja got her tunnel—just sixty years late.

Time robbed Breton of an arresting postscript to this piece of civic improvement. During the first rainstorm after the opening, water failed to drain away, turning the pubic triangle into a pond. For a city as house-proud as Paris, which spends more per head on sanitation than does any other conurbation in the world, such a fault could not be allowed to survive. Resignedly, the public works department ripped up the work, rebuilt the drainage system, and restored our square to its former state.

By the spring, I was coming to terms with France. Those months of isolation, physical and intellectual, had saved me. Instead of letting me choke on a cultural feast, Paris put me on a diet, spoon-feeding me its riches sip by sip.

Formerly incomprehensible objects and events became subjects of study. On my way to the *boulanger* for an early-morning baguette, I would pause to browse the day's supplies piled in front of the restaurant next door, their changes reflecting the passing of the seasons: green-gold olive oil from Provence; butter from Guérande, gritty with sea salt; oysters from the Atlantic coast, not—as in Australia—jumbled in sodden burlap bags but packed in boxes woven from paper-thin shavings of white wood. A few weeks later there would be the first yellow-red Napoléon cherries, prunes from Agen, and wheels of Saint-Nectaire cheese from the Auvergne region, their gray rind scumbled like the skin of a elephant.

Later in the morning, skirting the men from La Monnaie (the Mint) who congregated here every day to play *boules*, I would take a coffee at the café opposite.

On one such day, a couple holding a folded map stopped by me. The young man said, in halting French, "*Excusez-moi, monsieur . . .* the Sainte-Chapelle?"

I nodded toward the Palais de Justice. "It's on the other side. Take a left and the next right. You'll see the queue."

Just then the waiter brought my *express*, with the customary tumbler of water and sugar cubes wrapped in paper. Hand on hip, he looked after the walkers.

"Tourists!" he said, not unkindly.

I shrugged, as neighbors do, but I felt like Nick Carraway in *The Great Gatsby*, a stranger until someone even more out of his depth asked for directions: "I told him. And as I walked on I was lonely no longer. I was a guide, a pathfinder, an original settler. He had casually conferred on me the freedom of the neighborhood."

❋ · 5 · ❋

CHRISTMAS WITH KANGAROOS

Batemans Bay, New South Wales, Australia. December 1956. 34°C. Trailed around a wilting tree, Christmas lights blink wanly, paled to near invisibility by the sun that streams through curtains helpless to mute its glare. As flies circle, pine needles abandon the effort of attachment and drift down to join others littered on the sun-faded carpet.

ONE AUTUMN SOON AFTER I MOVED TO FRANCE, MARIE-DOMINIQUE and I took the car ferry to England. On the road to Calais we passed scores of people along the roadside, plastic bags in hand. They were scouring the grass for snails lured out by the moist, warm weather. Back home, the catch would be set out on beds of flour for a few days to cleanse their digestive systems, then baked with garlic, parsley, and butter to create a traditional dish of French cuisine.

Later that morning, we rolled off the ferry and headed for London. Around us, the landscape, the weather, and presumably the snails were identical with those of Picardy. Yet the verges of Kent were deserted.

The same would have been true had we driven into Germany, Switzerland, Italy, or Spain. Only Portugal rivaled France in appreciation of the delectable gastropod. And when it came to scouring the countryside for the freshest examples, the field was left largely to the French.

With the move to France I acquired a kind of double vision, an ability, sometimes troublesome but more often enlightening, to see and appreciate both the Gallic and Anglo ways of life. For the first time, the weather and the seasons, to which until then I'd barely given a thought, became elements in almost every decision I made, social, domestic, or professional.

In California, we had mostly ignored them. Cars were air-conditioned, as were the malls, cinemas, and offices to which we drove. An intimacy with parking facilities was a key to survival, and "Do you validate?" our mantra.

In food, seasonality didn't apply. Refrigeration meant that avocados, mangoes, and cherries, once available for only a few weeks each year, could be enjoyed anytime, and oysters eaten even in months without an "r" in them, traditionally off-limits as the period when they spawned.

For Australians, a lack of seasonal variation was nothing new. Weather there was largely academic. Sometimes it was hot, at other times hotter. Very occasionally, it was cold. Even less often, it rained. But except for the periodic bushfires, variations were minute. When the American writer Poe Ballantine characterized rural Nebraska as having only two seasons, "merciless summer and a fairly pleasant fall," he might have been talking about the corner of the outback where I was raised.

To further complicate things, the Australian seasons are reversed. But even in high summer, most people observed the holiday traditions of a wintry Europe. In 1980, eyebrows were collectively raised when Rolf Harris released "Six White Boomers," a song that proposed an Aussie Santa in a sleigh pulled not by reindeer but by kangaroos. No Dasher, Dancer, Prancer, Vixen, let alone red-nosed Rudolph? Unthinkable.

There was more than custom in our discomfort with a sunlit Christmas. Something deep in our cultural DNA revolted against the idea. British comedian David Mitchell wrote recently:

> When I was at university, we nearly put on a Christmas-themed summer revue. We were planning a sketch show to tour the country in July and August and were racking our brains for a theme when we got very excited about making it a Christmas show, with all the sketches about Christmas and a festively decorated set. . . . The show was to be called "Deep and Crisp and Even" and have a big picture of a snow-topped pizza on the posters. But none of our usual touring venues would take it.

I can understand why. To blot out visions of a snow-covered Christmas took an effort of will not everyone was prepared to make. While a few adventurous souls might celebrate Christmas in Australia with a picnic of lobster and fruit salad within hearing range of the surf, our family, faithful to the European tradition, sat down, perspiring, to roast turkey, brussels sprouts, potatoes, stuffing, and plum pudding with brandy butter.

When the queen broadcast her message on Christmas afternoon, we gathered around the TV to listen. A decade or two earlier it had been the radio, and grandfathers and a few older uncles even stood in respect. Such reverence for the lost British Empire, now reborn as the Commonwealth—Empire Lite—wasn't rare among that generation, many of whom still spoke of Britain as "home" even when they were born in Australia and had never visited England.

In those days, when theaters and cinemas played "God Save the Queen" after every show, it was an act of reckless courage not to rise to your feet and remain motionless until it finished. If you got through the door at the back of the cinema before the anthem began, you were exempt from this duty, so there was a scramble to leave before the prefatory roll of drums. One irate filmgoer wrote to a trade paper, "Last night, at my local cinema, I stood at the end of the screening for the national anthem. When I turned to leave, I found that the other patrons and even the staff had gone, and I was locked in."

Like the severed limb that still itched, the sense of a winter Christmas survived no matter to what corner of the world one was exiled. Be it in tundra or jungle, the traditional Christmas dinner would be eaten; the tree decorated; and the carol concerts, midnight mass, and readings or productions of Dickens's *A Christmas Carol* all take place. The seasons and their rituals cut deep.

California's embrace of the new had lulled me into thinking France would be the same. Instead I found it deeply respectful of the past, suspicious of the present, and downright skeptical about the future. Above all, it paid no attention to the rules governing the rest of the world. "The French believe that all errors are distant, someone else's fault," wrote the social critic Adam Gopnik. My new neighbors and in-laws listened to only one voice: that of what they called *le patrimoine*—"the heritage"—the accumulated glory of France.

❈ · 6 · ❈

THE SEINE IN FLOOD

Paris 6me. January 2018. 3 a.m. Rain all week, a silent drizzle, shining the metal roofs of the city grayer; a rain invisible at night but audible in the tattoo of fat drops falling six stories from the gutters to smash on the court-yard cobbles. Out of sight but less than a kilometer away, the Seine rises, invading the bankside promenades.

FEBRUARY 2018, AND THE SEINE HAS SELDOM BEEN HIGHER. OF the bridges under which scores of barges and pleasure boats pass daily, only a narrow space remains above water. Beneath the Pont de l'Alma, the seventeen-foot statue of a Zouave, a rifleman from a North African regiment, stands resolutely on guard. When the waters are high Parisians say, "The Zouave's feet must be wet." Today, they lap his beard.

Friends overseas email, "Are you all right? Have the floodwa-ters reached you yet?" Wondering if they know something I don't, I go out on the terrace and look down six stories into our street. No water there except on the wet pavement, where sanitation workers hose it down in their twice-weekly tour.

After lunch, I take a walk down to the river. Streets on the southern, or left, bank of the Seine are at little risk of being flooded. Rising from the river to the long ridge of Montparnasse, the ground here is mostly the sandstone that has been quarried for centuries to build the city.

People on the right bank are not so fortunate. A flat river basin, its clay soil and a high water table make it prone to flooding. Engineers constructing the Opéra in the 1860s had to run pumps day and night to keep the foundations dry. When they stopped, water seeped in, inspiring the legend that a lake lay under the building across which a mutilated musical genius—the phantom of the Opéra—poled.

Looking at the Seine today, I can believe such myths. In yellow-gray spate, the water is inching up the stone wall toward street level. The previous year, the town hall posted online an alarming computer simulation of what would happen if it spilled over. Not only the metro stations and underground parking garages would flood, but so would the basements of the Grand Palais and the Louvre.

It had happened before. In January 1910 the Seine rose eight meters, only three more than today, invading even the lower streets on our side of the river. The river didn't need to brim its banks. Once rain filled the sewer and stormwater outlets, pressure from the river acted as a pump, sending water spouting out of manholes and drains. Markers on older buildings indicate the level reached by *la crue de la Seine du 28 janvier 1910*: anything from knee to shoulder height. There's an element of bravado in such memorials. *You think* your *river floods? Take a look at this!*

The Zouave on the Pont de l'Alma.

For a time, the writer Anaïs Nin lived on a houseboat, *La Belle Aurore*, moored on the right bank. Enamored of water and journeys, Nin fancied herself on a cruise without end, with new adventures forever floating downriver toward her. "Once inside the houseboat," she wrote, "all the voyages began. Even at night with its shutters closed, no smoke coming out of its chimney, asleep and secret, it had an air of mysteriously sailing somewhere." But weather is no respecter of literature. Today, her former mooring is lost under a racing torrent.

Confined between stone walls, the Seine here is unrecognizable as the same river it is upstream, where the water is free to find its own level. Novelist William Wharton, who also lived on a houseboat— moored at Le Port-Marly, about twenty kilometers outside the city—returned from a weekend away to find the river in flood:

> The beautiful black or green Seine is a raging yellow muddy river now; it looks like the Amazon, with rippling waves as the water courses along its rampaging way. It has covered the island across from us so that it looks like one huge wild river with whitecaps all the way to the bank on the other side of the island. Our neighbors are running around like crazy people, fastening things down and cursing us for abandoning our boat.

Wharton and his houseboat survived, but each time the river runs high it carries fragments of shattered lifestyles downstream.

During the high water of 2018, the staff of the riverside Shake-speare & Company bookshop warned customers to expect the

> bizarre and revealing sight of the quays strewn with all the manmade flotsam and organic life that is usually borne through the city and downriver beneath the glaucous, roping waters, unseen by us surface dwellers. Stranded items spotted near the bookshop in June 2016 included an ornate wingback armchair, countless tons of riverweed, and a full *peloton* [platoon] of algae-furred bicycles!

The rushing torrent seemingly just under my feet, I cross the Pont des Arts, the fragile-looking metal bridge on stone piers that leads to the Louvre. Of the thirty-seven bridges that suture one half of Paris to the other, this one is most richly encrusted with emotion. It takes the form of *cadenas d'amour*: "love locks." Couples write their names on a small brass padlock, attach it to a security barrier, and toss the key into the river. So many *cadenas* accumulated on the Pont des Arts that barriers tore loose from their weight. In 2015 the city removed forty-five tons of locks and replaced the metal mesh with glass, but the fad still flourishes.

Cross any bridge over the Seine and there's a brief sense of hovering between worlds. To Guillaume Apollinaire, the bridges' wayward characters and tendency to develop personalities of their own recalled sheep. In his poem "Zone," he wrote, "Shepherdess O Eiffel Tower this morning the bridges are bleating." The image of indiscipline reflects the bridges' ambiguous status; technically belonging to Paris, they are administered and maintained by the state as part of the *patrimoine*.

Filmmakers often use Paris bridges to imply links between different worlds. In *Last Tango in Paris*, Marlon Brando and Maria Schneider independently cross the unglamorous Pont de Bir-Hakeim, which celebrates a little-known battle of 1942, en route to the soulless, bourgeois apartment where they have their erotic encounters. For *Munich*, Steven Spielberg imagined the same bridge hosting a produce market, where the Mossad assassin played by Eric Bana meets Mathieu Amalric to bargain for information while doing the weekend shopping. Bana, a keen cook in the film, advises Amalric on seasonal vegetables as they discuss political murder—shorthand for the banality of contemporary terrorism.

Cary Grant and Audrey Hepburn pass under this and a dozen other bridges during their nocturnal rendezvous on a *bateau mouche* in *Charade*. The operator spices up that voyage by spotlighting lovers as they cuddle and grope along the stone-paved riverbank, the same one where Gene Kelly dances with Leslie Caron in *An American in Paris* to "Love Is Here to Stay" and Goldie Hawn defies gravity to float above Woody Allen's head as she sings "I'm Through with Love" in *Everyone Says I Love You*. All underwater now. Fortunately romance isn't soluble.

One of the stranger works of transpontine art was the 2006 collaboration between conceptual artist Sophie Calle and architect Frank Gehry. It took the form of a plastic telephone booth

Sophie Calle and Frank Gehry's phone booth on the Pont du Garigliano.

resembling, typically for Paris, a gaudy, exotic flower. It stood on the Pont du Garigliano, one of the less stylish bridges (though, because of its height of eleven meters above the water, popular with suicides). Inside the booth, a metal plate explained: "My name is Sophie Calle. You are standing in my phone booth. Only I know the number. I will dial it from time to time, but completely out of the blue, in the hope that someone will answer."

Would Ms. Calle have placed such a box on London Bridge or the Brooklyn Bridge? Did anyone ever participate in a conversation with her over that phone? It hardly matters. The booth celebrates chance and its multitude of possibilities, but also Paris, its bridges, and the capacity of both to welcome and nurture the unexpected.

Watching the Seine swirl around a bridge's stone piers, one understands the erotic appeal of death by water that inspired American poet and onetime Paris expatriate Hart Crane. In his cycle "Voyages," he wrote, "sleep, death, desire, / Close round one instant in one floating flower." One night in 1932, he leaped from a boat into the Gulf of Mexico. His body was never found.

The lure of Paris's bridges feels strongest on the oldest, the so-called Pont Neuf, or New Bridge, which *was* new once, when work concluded in 1607 under Henry IV. His statue stands proudly at the point where the bridge transects the Île de la Cité. So often has it been disassembled for repairs that each stone is numbered, ensuring that it's put back exactly as built.

Below and behind it, on a triangle of grass and trees called Vert-Galant, one is closer to the Seine than anywhere else in Paris. Once the Île aux Juifs, or Jews' Island, it was here that Jacques de Molay, grand master of the Knights Templar, and his lieutenant Geoffroy de Charnay were burned at the stake in March 1314, and from where the ashes of Guy Debord, who formulated the discipline known as psychogeography, were, as he asked, consigned to the Seine.

Yet the presiding spirit of Vert-Galant isn't any of these but a girl whose corpse was fished out of the river nearby, sometime in the 1880s. A cast of her calm, almost dreamy face, christened L'Inconnue de la Seine (the Unknown Girl of the Seine), inspired novels, stories, and poems. Proving that history repeats itself first as tragedy, then as farce, L'Inconnue enjoyed an unexpected modern reincarnation: in the 1950s Norwegian toymaker Asmund Laerdal chose hers as the face of Resusci Anne, the plastic figure used to demonstrate mouth-to-mouth resuscitation. Since then, more than three hundred million people have kissed those dead lips.

I SPY STRANGERS

*Kings Cross, Sydney, Australia. October 1986. 9 p.m.
28°C. Slot machines subside in the Returned Soldiers
Club and hands are laid on hearts as a recorded voice
intones, "They shall grow not old, as we that are left
grow old." At the back door, the stink from a garbage
bag gravid with rotting shrimp shells blends with the
cloying scent of frangipani flowers.*

THE SENSE OF NATIONAL DESTINY THAT DRIVES THE FRENCH HAS
no equivalent in my native Australia. Its history as a dumping
ground for Britain's jailbirds, followed by centuries of colonial
rule, induces a sense of inferiority that feels bred-in-the-bone.
We're taught from childhood to suppress all inclinations to self-
importance. Few people are less graceful in accepting a compli-
ment. In an extremity of pride at some achievement, we might at
most mumble, "It's all right."

From shunning self-advertisement, it was a short step to believing we had nothing to boast about. This seemed confirmed by the
quality of the celebrities who visited us. Rarely could any performer

in his or her prime be persuaded to spend twenty-four hours on a plane simply to play our few meager venues. Local showmen complained, "We only get them on the way up or the way down."

So when, in the 1980s, the University of Sydney asked for my help in attracting overseas buyers to a trade fair for documentary filmmakers, I was sure some incentive would be needed to coax executives from their Beverly Hills and Manhattan offices to our insignificant shores.

What better than our lifestyle, in particular our beaches? A visit to the relevant politicians proved surprisingly productive of both encouragement and funds. Accordingly, we were able to offer every distributor who attended a week's holiday, all expenses paid, on Australia's most popular natural wonder, the Great Barrier Reef.

Braced for a stampede of freeloaders who would grab the holiday but skip the fair, we watched in confusion as our guests diligently attended the fair but declined the bonus. All had businesses to run and were anxious to get back to them. If they wanted sun, sand, and seafood, all were available closer to home, at their condos in Florida. A sterner imperative dominated their consciousness: Who's minding the store?

We were guilty of what sociologists were calling "cultural cringe," an assumption that nothing in Australian culture could possibly interest a sophisticated foreigner. In our defense, the strategy was already being embraced by the minister who funded our initiative. Hoping to lure college graduates from northern Europe, his department produced some embarrassing posters showing their dream candidate—young, male, and white—standing on a beach in mortarboard, academic gown, and swimming trunks.

The film-fair experience made me cautious in dealing with the few European intellectuals who did make it to Sydney. If American businessmen scorned our natural inducements, how much more contemptuous would be these men, marinated in the art and thought of France, Germany, and Italy?

So it was a jolt when, meeting the distinguished French documentary filmmaker Jean Rouch off the plane to attend a conference on ethnographic film in the Pacific region, I had to help him retrieve the surfboard he'd checked through as excess baggage. On the drive to his hotel, he explained he'd learned to surf while making a film about the Gulf of Guinea and was eager to sample the point break at Bondi Beach.

Not long after, film director Josef von Sternberg agreed to be a guest of the Sydney Film Festival. Visiting him in one of the city's most staid hotels, I found his suite filled with New Guinean tribal artifacts he'd acquired by cleaning out most of the city's dealers in ethnic art. Seeing the thrones surmounted with human skulls and clubs edged with shark teeth, I couldn't help recalling "Hot Voodoo," an outrageous dance number in his 1932 film *Blonde Venus*. A line of dusky chorus girls leads onstage a gorilla in chains who, on shedding its skin, proves to be Marlene Dietrich in a blond wig, sequins, and not much else. No need to cringe about antipodean culture in von Sternberg's presence. He'd embraced it with vigor.

Umberto Eco, the Italian literary critic, novelist, and inspired

Marlene Dietrich in Josef von Sternberg's Blonde Venus.

language theorist, was the greatest surprise of all. After we'd seemed to bond during an interview, I gambled that the academics who'd asked him to their conference would be too awed to invite him to dinner, and so I did. He accepted with flattering enthusiasm.

Suppressing the tendency to book at some Europeanized five-star establishment, I chose a harborside eatery whose tumbledown exterior belied its reputation for fresh seafood. Eco proved as jolly and unconventional as his roly-poly build suggested. Far from shunning Australia's enticements, he confessed he'd only agreed to attend the conference if its organizers threw in a week on the Great Barrier Reef.

Umberto Eco.

He described with glee how, descending late one morning from his hotel room on an island resort, he expressed a wish for some oysters before lunch. "No worries, mate," said the concierge. Handing him a small hammer, he directed him to the foreshore, where Eco could help himself from those that festooned the rocks.

At the time, Eco was best known for his first novel, *The Name of the Rose*, which shrewdly used the frame of a murder mystery to embody an inquiry into the nature of medieval religious thought. It became an international bestseller and a movie starring Sean Connery.

He didn't apologize for working both sides of the intellectual street. "At my age," he told me, expertly shelling a shrimp, "a scholar has two alternatives—to write a novel, or to run off to the French Riviera with a showgirl. I decided to write the novel . . ." He paused to suck the juice from a shrimp head; I tried not to flinch. ". . . but that's not to say I may not, one day, exercise the second option."

Meeting Eco, Rouch, von Sternberg, and others like them raised the corner of a curtain on a very different Europe from the one I had imagined. A fellow science-fiction writer once said of Arthur C. Clarke, author of *2001: A Space Odyssey*, that "his preferred future was extremely [H. G.] Wellsian, full of brainy people sitting about in togas swapping theorems." This was my vision of Europe. Maybe not togas exactly, but definitely a high seriousness. So when European intellectuals behaved like ordinary men and women, I suspected them of acting the fool for our benefit, celebrating the trivial to prove they were Just Regular Guys.

It took a while to realize that Rouch's surfing, von Sternberg's artifacts, and Eco's novels represented a different way of looking at the world. Eco didn't eat our seafood out of politeness; he genuinely liked it. Nor did he turn up his nose at our writers and thinkers, many of whom he found bracing and original. Just because our way of life was different didn't necessarily mean it was inferior. Until I met these men, my aim in life had been to, one day, live in Los Angeles. Now I had doubts. Might Europe, despite its daunting traditions, be the better option? Did London, Rome, even Paris offer more than madrigals, dreaming spires, old masters, and the rustle of ancient pages reverently turned?

❉ · 8 · ❉

GETTING TO KNOW THE FRENCH

Place de la Concorde, Paris 8me. May 2017. 6 a.m. 10°C. As fountains splash and wet cobbles gleam in the slanting morning sun, tankers painted the somber green of all Paris sanitation vehicles trundle around its largest square, flushing its gutters as if in hopes of sluicing away the blood of those thousands of victims of La Terreur, a king and queen included, who died here. For a year after, not even dogs would cross it, so overpowering was the stench.

That Marie-Dominique should, in her thirties, have decided to marry and, in doing so, chosen a foreigner surprised and, in some cases, alarmed the people around her.

After a number of near misses over the years, her family and friends had decided that buzzing around the world as she did on assignment as a journalist, she was far too busy to settle down. They had her categorized as the glamorous aunt or niece, always good for a generous gift at a wedding or christening and free at a moment's notice to join a Tuscan house party or help crew a yacht sailing to the Bahamas.

Who was I, an unknown, to have caught this highflier and coaxed her back to earth? Invitations to their home aren't something the French make lightly, but during my first few months in Paris we were guests at several dinners where eating and drinking took second place to sizing me up.

Christmas with my new family had alerted me of what to expect. Fortunately, that went off well because I told a story about the misadventures of an Australian friend, the writer George Johnston, in the vineyards of Bordeaux just after World War II. Watching them smile at his floundering—and my own, in trying to tell the story in my fumbling French—taught me that the rules governing social life in Los Angeles would not do for France.

The passport to social acceptance in most societies is novelty. In California I played the slightly disoriented Englishman, increasing the broadness of my vowels and saying, when offered coffee, "I don't suppose you have any tea?"

That would never do in France, where all things and people are judged according to the degree with which they share French values and ideals. Fortunately I had learned enough about both to, if not contribute, then at least nod in the right places.

At one such dinner party, the conversation turned to honeymoons and the fact that Marie-Dominique and I were too busy to have one.

"There's a good story," I said, "in the memoirs of Giscard d'Estaing . . ."

The autobiography of the former French president had just been translated into English, and my knowledge of it extended only as far as an extract published by one of the British papers. In it, he described his first meeting with British prime minister Margaret Thatcher. It took place in Paris, at the Hôtel de Crillon, which looks out on Place de la Concorde.

Not sure with what kind of woman he was dealing, the urbane Giscard let her lecture him about Franco-British relations. As she did so, his mind wandered. Looking out on the sunlit fountains of Concorde, he wondered how many young couples had enjoyed this view on the first morning of their marriage. Why, he himself—

Seized by surprise, he interrupted Thatcher in mid-discourse.

"Forgive me, Madame Prime Minister," he said. "I was just thinking how many young couples spent the first night of their honeymoon at the Crillon. I did so myself, but it's only in this instant that I realized it was *in this very suite!*"

If he expected an answering smile, some sentimental response, he was disappointed. Raising one eyebrow in irritation, Mrs. Thatcher continued her recital. Clearly, the nickname "the Iron Lady" was well earned, an insight that affected all Giscard's subsequent negotiations with her.

"Well, here is a surprise," said our host when I finished the story. "A visitor who knows something of our country that, in my case at least, is quite new."

Said over a dinner in Australia, a society preoccupied with equality, this would almost certainly have been sarcastic, and intended as an insult. In that egalitarian society, nobody was less appreciated than the know-it-all who soiled the garden of ignorance with an unwelcome factoid. In France, however, it was said with sincerity, even respect.

After that, I felt a lot easier about playing the heritage card, which is how I found myself on a balcony one night overlooking the Canal Saint-Martin, chatting about calendars with a man I'd only just met.

Inside, the party was getting noisy, but out here the air was heavy with odors of vegetal decay from the sluggish water of the canal—what the British poet Rupert Brooke called "the thrilling, sweet and rotten, / Unforgettable, unforgotten / River-smell." They blended seamlessly with the cigar being smoked by someone a few meters along the balcony.

"It is too early for heat like this," the smoker said from the darkness. "Every year, the summer comes earlier and stays longer."

Groping for something more than bland agreement, I remembered a conversation with Céline years before, about how during the French Revolution, someone had the idea of renaming the months of the year. Thermidor was one; Brumaire was another, and what was the Month of Fruit . . . ?

"I know what you mean," I said. "This is Fructidor, but it's more like Vendémiaire."

The red coal of the burning cigar moved closer, faintly illuminating the face of the smoker. Glasses, a beard . . . and, unexpectedly, a clerical collar.

"I knew you were a *cinéaste*, m'sieur. Are you also an historian?"

"No. Just interested."

"In the *Calendrier républicain?*" He chuckled. "Believe me, my friend, you are in the minority. Hardly any of my own countrymen have ever heard of it. Or of Fabre d'Églantine."

The name was new to me too, but I risked a bluff. "Not exactly a name one forgets."

"So *he* thought," said the man. He shifted his cigar and held out his hand. "Adrian de Grandpré. Of course, you know he faked it."

Backpedaling, I said hurriedly, "I'm really no expert . . ." But it was too late.

Some time later, as I stepped back into the room, Marie-Dominique joined me. "What were you talking about on the terrace? You were out there for an hour."

"The weather, as a matter of fact."

I transferred to the pocket of my jacket the two pages of scribbled notes dictated by my new acquaintance and his list of books for further reading,

"What's all that?" she asked.

"Would you believe . . . homework?"

9

AS IF IT WERE YESTERDAY

A truck stop outside Poitiers. August 2010. 11 a.m. 22°C. Heat sucks moisture from the skin and desiccates the mouth. Kids, fully clothed, run squealing through the mist of a brumisateur. *Feeling faintly foolish, I follow at a sober adult pace into a delicious rush of wet and cold. (Is this what a skydiver feels as he plummets through a cloud?) As I unlock the car a few minutes later, my clothes are just-ironed dry.*

MODESTO, CALIFORNIA, HOMETOWN OF *STAR WARS* CREATOR George Lucas, could have been Junee in New South Wales, where I grew up. The table-flat landscape; the ubiquitous pickups; the locals lounging on benches, time on their hands and nothing on their minds; the railway line cutting the town in two; the freight trains that clanked through the level crossing, damming back traffic on each side—I knew them all. Lucas's alter ego, Luke Skywalker, spoke for us both when he said of his home planet, Tatooine: "If there's a bright center to the universe, you're on the planet that it's farthest from."

For proof that weather and landscape influence behavior, look no further than the similarities between countries with similar ecologies. Anyone who has lived in a community like Modesto, never mind its nationality, will tell you that the perception of days and weeks stretches or shrinks with the season, time flowing faster or slower in accordance with the degree of heat or cold.

Our brains know that time is elastic. A mild electrical current applied to the right inferior frontal cortex changes our sense of duration. A sustained lack of sunlight can induce depression. Why should stifling humidity or Arctic cold not have a similar effect?

Older societies adjusted their system of measurement to physical circumstances. The Persians measured distances not in kilometers but in parasangs, an elastic term representing how far one could walk in an hour in the local terrain. The rougher the country, the shorter the parasang. A "New York minute" is the parasang writ small. It recognizes that in a busy city, time speeds up—something even Einstein understood: a light-year, after all, is a parasang at the opposite end of the scale.

In a lifetime spent in Anglo-Saxon countries, I'd experienced a succession of seismic social and artistic changes: the Beat Generation, 1968 and the student revolution, flower power, Woodstock. After each, we brushed ourselves off, burned our banners, gave our outdated T-shirts to Goodwill, and moved on.

An acceptance of this fluid lifestyle had governed my life in California, where each day one woke alert for the Next Big Thing. But I felt no such urgency in France. Within its cultural microclimate, time moved at a different speed, sometimes even running in reverse or circling back on itself. I began to doubt my former commitment to the future. California found no merit in dwelling on the past, whereas France seemed to do little else.

In 1988, the French government commissioned a statue to mark the centenary of the wrongful conviction for treason of army officer Alfred Dreyfus, framed in a shameful example of an endemic anti-Semitism. Almost four meters tall, the statue depicted an officer saluting with a broken sword. The surface of the figure was bubbled, as if it had been dipped in pitch, then set on fire.

Minister of Culture Jack Lang wanted it erected on the parade ground of the École Militaire, the military college where Dreyfus was ritually disgraced before being deported to Devil's Island. The army blocked its placement in so sensitive a location. ("My dear sir, are you aware that even Napoléon graduated from here?") Banished to the Tuileries Garden, it stood for years in an obscure corner, facing a blank wall. Rehabilitated in 1994, it found a permanent home in a tiny park on boulevard Raspail, on the edge of Montparnasse.

When Louise was little I would walk her to school, past the park. We watched workmen construct a base and maneuver the heavy bronze figure into place. That was on a Friday. When we returned on Monday, somebody had spray-painted a word on the stone plinth.

Louise stopped and spelled it out. "What does this mean, Papa?"

"I'm not sure. Come on, *chérie*. We'll be late."

The word was *traître*. "Traitor."

In France, the past, like the weather, was ever with us—for good or ill.

Statue of Alfred Dreyfus by Louis Mittelberg.

Learning to be papa. With Louise, age five.

10

STORMY MONDAY

Versailles. February 1990. 10 a.m. Wind drones in the trees. A white-haired guardian hides in a Perspex box the size of a telephone booth. From the woods on either side of the road come rushing cracks. "The trees are falling!" he yells over the noise, in a sort of glee. "Marie Antoinette couldn't do it. Louis Quatorze couldn't do it. But they are coming down now!"

ONE FEBRUARY MORNING IN MY FIRST YEAR IN PARIS, I WOKE IN our tiny apartment on the Île de la Cité to the rattling of windows. Icy air billowed white net curtains into the room. Shivering, I pushed the French windows closed and, through the glass, looked out onto Place Dauphine two floors below.

For days a gray fog had shrouded the city, composed, I decided, of one part water vapor, one part automobile exhaust, and the rest smoke from unfiltered Gauloises cigarettes.

Overnight, however, the fog had disappeared, driven off by a wind straight from the steppes of Russia. Across the square, our neighbor, Monsieur Gruyere, had brought his dog, Snowy, down for the customary canine reasons. Both now huddled in the doorway, Gruyere with hands shoved deep in the pockets of the coral-and-lime tracksuit he'd pulled on over his pajamas.

For Snowy, peering out from between his ankles, desperate need battled dislike of the wind. Finally he darted out, performed a sketchy pee next to a tree, gave a perfunctory flick with one rear paw, and fled back to shelter.

"There's a storm," I said, crawling back into bed.

"It'll go away," Marie-Dominique mumbled.

But it didn't. When we got up at nine a.m., the wind was a steady drone overhead. It lashed the leafless chestnut trees below our windows and propelled the few pedestrians across the square like scraps of newspaper. According to the news, the wind had blown all night across most of central and northern France. Trees were down, houses had lost their roofs, and on TV the *speakerines* were using words like *ouragan*.

Mention of damage to houses had Marie-Dominique on the phone to her mother.

I understood almost none of their conversation, but her repeated troubled looks at the sky were graphic enough.

"*Maman* is worried about the house in Richebourg," she said. "If one of those big trees fell on the roof, it would be a disaster. She wants us to go there and check."

"How would we get there?" Richebourg had no railway connection. The nearest station was twenty kilometers away.

"By car, *évidemment*."

On the TV, I watched as a caravan was crumpled against a tree like a sodden shoebox. The image shifted to a six-story apartment building under construction. As its scaffolding collapsed in the storm, sheets of metal went spinning like playing cards and industrial-strength PVC ripped like toilet paper.

"You're sure it's safe?" I asked.

Marie-Dominique spared the screen a glance. "This is all from farther south. It's nowhere near that bad in the west."

I was to get to know this tone of voice well, and learn not to argue with it. When it comes to family, world war alone takes precedence, and then only if the enemy is actually at the gates.

"Well, let's go, if we're going," I said. "If it gets any worse, I'd prefer to be under cover."

I had, I must admit, a hidden agenda. The road to Richebourg passed Versailles. So far I'd been put off visiting the palace and its gardens by the tourists that crowded both, but weather like this might keep them in their hotels.

Even as we reached the Seine, the force of the wind was alarming. It jammed houseboats against the stone abutments, and down by the Pont d'Iéna, where the *bateaux mouches* excursion boats docked, men struggled to slide shut their big windows before the storm blew them out.

Taking the *Périphérique*, the ring road enclosing Paris, we crossed the Seine at Saint-Cloud and climbed into Ville-d'Avray, the beginnings of the countryside. Torn twigs littered the road. Trees thrashed in the gale. A few had been levered out of the ground like rotten teeth.

Medieval engraving of a hurricane.

The few drivers who passed us clutched their steering wheels and stared ahead with a concentration uncharacteristic of French motorists, who can, while at the wheel, speak on a mobile phone, eat a baguette *jambon-fromage*, and make love, sometimes all three at once.

Nobody else turned off to Versailles. We drove through the town almost alone and skirted the vast park. High spiked railings barred the common people from this synthetic world of lawns, forests, and boating lakes, private theaters, fountains, and pavilions. Within this bubble of privilege, a succession of French kings and their wives and mistresses had lived in a style that might have been copied from a canvas by Poussin or Claude Lorrain.

But today the gardens were deserted. It was as if the same gale that swept us here had blown away the five thousand people who'd lived in and around the palace at the time of Louis XVI and Marie Antoinette.

We drove through the unmanned main gate and down a wide avenue toward the park entrance. At the foot of the drive, the road ended in a lake. The wind shredded the flow of the fountains and bent almost horizontal the plumes of water that once played above the gardens of André Le Nôtre. Under the scudding clouds, we were alone but exhilarated, infected by the same madness.

Obviously this was no day for sightseeing. Thirty minutes later, we were back on the road. A giant beech, in falling, had hammered a car flat. A gendarme directed us around the wreck. At Richebourg the wind had uprooted one of the giant poplars, but though branches and leaves littered the garden, the house itself was safe. Next door a redwood had snapped in half, exposing dense wood, blood red.

We hid inside the house, not even taking down the heavy wooden shutters and hardly daring to turn on the lights, as if they might attract the wrath of the storm. Twenty-eight people died in France that weekend, and many more in the rest of western Europe, but we were oblivious. That night, in a wide bed tucked into an alcove surrounded by tall shelves of books, as the wind slammed at the shutters, our daughter, Louise, was conceived, a child of the hurricane.

11

TOCK...TOCK...TOCK...

Church of Saint-Sulpice, Paris 5me. July 1994. 2 p.m.
12°C. Afternoon light, tinted an oceanic chartreuse by
the stained-glass windows, spotlights the dust, which
swirls in a Brownian movement each time it's agitated
anew by the thump of the wooden door admitting yet
another tourist. As each new arrival fails to remove his
hat or make the sign of the cross, the holy-water fonts,
created from two halves of a giant clamshell, evert
their silver lips in contempt.

U MBERTO ECO WOULD HAVE APPROVED OF MY DECISION TO MOVE
to Paris to join the woman I loved. After all, hadn't I in a sense just
chosen his second option, and instead of writing a novel, run off
with a chorus girl?

That was certainly how it appeared to people in Los Angeles.
One of the acquaintances I'd made there, more bitter than the rest,
growled, "Is this what you do? Come to town, make friends, then
leave?" Of my apologetic explanation of a whirlwind romance,
which the French call a *coup de foudre*, "thunderclap," they were as

incredulous as the director's assistant in *Day for Night*—François Truffaut's fable about the tribulations of moviemaking—when she learns that the star's girlfriend has decamped with a stuntman. "I can see leaving a guy for a movie," she says, "but leaving a movie for a *guy . . . ?* "

Though not by intention, Eco also provided another clue to the puzzle of France. In 1988 he published a second novel, *Foucault's Pendulum*. I read it in Los Angeles, soon losing myself in its winding byways, its alleys of speculation, its cabinets of mystical curiosities, and its rag-and-bone markets of occult lore. Eco wrote once that "entering a novel is like going on a climb in the mountains; you have to learn the rhythm of respiration, acquire the pace; otherwise you stop right away." I made it to the end of *Foucault's Pendulum*, but not without a sense of having conquered a literary Everest.

The novel begins in a vast building in Paris, where a wire, attached high in a dome, supports the pendulum of the title, a weight that swings back and forth ceaselessly above some sort of mystical diagram sunk into the marble floor.

Eco specifies a wire sixty-seven meters long and a pendulum weighing twenty-eight kilograms. Only a cathedral could accommodate something so cumbersome, and even if some archbishop agreed to house it, the chaos among his worshippers could only be imagined; one visualized whole pews full of parishioners mowed down by its swing. And what use would such a device fulfill? In the novel, it somehow proves that the earth rotates. The whole thing was obviously one of the wilder flights of Eco's imagination.

On one of our first walks around Paris the spring after I arrived, Marie-Dominique and I strolled up to the highest point of the Left Bank. It's dominated by an enormous building of ecclesiastical character with an imposing Roman-style colonnade.

"What church is that?" I asked.

"It's not a church," said Marie-Dominique. "It's the Panthéon."

When I looked blank, she continued, "In London, great poets are buried under the floor of Westminster Abbey? Well, this is our version. All sorts of people are buried in the crypt. Voltaire, Rousseau, Zola, Dumas, Hugo, the Curies. Even Jean Moulin, the resistance leader—though his body was never found."

"What did they bury, then?"

"An empty coffin, I suppose. The same with Antoine de Saint-Exupéry. His plane crashed in the sea. The body isn't the point, it's the *idea* . . ." Seeing my interest, she asked, "Do you want to go in?"

"Sure." (How different everything might have been had I refused. For one thing, you would not be reading this book.) We walked up the steps, through the Corinthian columns with their acanthus-leaf capitals, under the inscription *"Aux grands hommes, la patrie reconnaissante"*—roughly "The homeland is grateful to its great men"—paid our admission, collected a brochure, and entered the vast, domed space.

I should have been admiring the heroic statuary, twice life-size, or the murals celebrating the achievements of France's past. Instead my eyes fixed on something across the marble floor: a circular diagram, above which lazily swung a golden sphere supported by a wire stretching out of sight overhead.

"It's the pendulum!"

Marie-Dominique looked puzzled. "Yes. *Le pendule de Foucault.* So?"

"But I thought . . ."

"What?"

"Never mind." To confess I believed that Umberto Eco made it up would just add to her doubts as to whether she'd made the right decision about me.

As she left to admire the murals, I rapidly skimmed the brochure.

The Panthéon started life as a cathedral, but because the revolution of 1789 disapproved of religion, it was never consecrated. Instead it became a shrine to the nation's great thinkers and creators. France could hardly have had a better symbol than a temple dedicated to secular saints. Unlike Rome, Paris was never a sacred city. Almost all its monuments are to intellect and reason, not the soul of man but his mind.

In 1855 a physicist named Léon Foucault, looking for a way to demonstrate visually that the earth rotates, was given permission to fix a pendulum to a swivel in the Panthéon dome. On the floor below, he laid out a 360-degree diagram, like the face of a compass. As the pendulum swung through an unvarying ten-second arc, independent of the earth's motion, the diagram itself seemed to move, making a complete turn every thirty-two hours.

Foucault's pendulum in 1851.

In 1633 Galileo, forced by the Inquisition to recant his findings that the earth revolved around the sun, was said to have muttered defiantly, *"E pur si muove"* (it still moves). Watching Foucault's experiment, one savant said in satisfaction, "At last Galileo is vindicated!"

To Eco, it said something profound about the French. "The Pendulum told me," he wrote, "that, as everything moved—earth, solar system, nebulae and black holes, all the children of the great cosmic expansion—one single point stood still: a pivot, bolt, or hook around which the universe could move."

And that single point was here, in Paris.

Was this what the French believed also? That Paris was the hub around which all else revolved? That their values were somehow cosmic, rooted deep in the actual creation of the universe—values that went so deep and were so stubbornly held that nothing could shake them?

Perhaps the things we found most infuriating about the French— their refusal to accommodate other nations, their insistence on favoring the national good over that of the world, their fidelity to their language and culture—were also those we secretly envied.

Is that what drew us here? Was Paris, in some mystical sense, the perfection to which we all aspired?

I thought of running the idea past Marie-Dominique but decided against it. What if she replied "Of course!"?

12

BABY TIME

Outside Helsinki, Finland. February 1971. 2 a.m. 4 degrees below zero C. The low sun, faint and yellow as a streetlamp, glimmers on the ice of a frozen lake and a slope crusted white with frost. A pump chugs at the foot of a jetty, keeping a few square meters free of ice and inviting the suicidal to plunge into the roiling black water. Instead, skin steaming and numbed by sauna heat, we roll naked in snow as soft and warm as wool.

A FEW YEARS PASSED BEFORE I GOT BACK TO FRENCH HISTORY. Understanding the 1789 revolution and oddities like the Republican calendar took a backseat to learning, in middle age, how to be a father.

Nothing widens one's understanding of a society like having a child. Though I didn't realize this till later, some of what parenthood taught me would leak back into my search for Fabre d'Églantine.

In fact, I date my first insight to the day we visited the clinic where our daughter would be delivered. Formerly a hunting lodge of Emperor Napoléon III, it stood in baroque splendor amid the remnants of a gracious garden in the upmarket suburb of Neuilly. Framed letters of recommendation decorated the walls of the waiting room. The first I read began, under a gilded letterhead incorporating a royal crest, "His Serene Highness wishes to thank the staff . . ." I didn't look at the rest.

Leading us on a tour of inspection, a lady in an elegant black dress opened the door to what she called "the finest delivery suite in Paris." She did not exaggerate. Three deep armchairs were ranged around the foot of a huge bed draped with a satin baldachin and clearly fit for a crowned head, or at least the child on whose head the crown would eventually rest.

Dazzled, we signed up, only to see Louise born in a perfectly adequate modern facility at the other end of the building. Apparently only the most serene of highnesses rated the five-star suite.

At the end of that first tour we were handed over to the anesthetist, who took down all our particulars, then asked when the baby was due. When we told him the estimated date of delivery, toward the end of September, he looked dubious.

"Not a good idea," he said. "That weekend, all our doctors will be away."

"Why?" Marie-Dominique asked. "Is there some kind of conference?"

"No, no conference," he said. "It's Yom Kippur. And also the first day of the skiing season."

At first I thought he was joking, but his expression was serious.

"And . . . that *matters*?" I said.

He shrugged. "Certainly, if you don't want your child delivered by the gardener."

In a cab back into town, I said, "The *skiing* season? Can you believe that?"

"Yes, it seemed early to me too," Marie-Dominique said. "When I used to ski, the lifts didn't open much before November." She looked at me sideways. "What, you think it's unusual that all the doctors would take the weekend off?"

"Well . . . a little. I hope it doesn't happen too often."

"Depends on what you mean by 'often.'" She ticked off dates on her fingers. "There's Christmas and the Réveillon—New Year's. After that, Good Friday in April isn't an official holiday, but most people take it off. Easter Monday falls about the middle of April. Labor Day on May 1. Eighth of May—Victory in Europe. The Ascension in May. Pentecost in June, Bastille Day July 14, the Assumption on the fifteenth of August, Yom Kippur, of course, at the end of September, All Saints' Day on November 1, and Armistice Day on November 11 . . ."

I opened my mouth to express astonishment, but she wasn't finished.

"When any holiday falls on a Tuesday or Thursday, we usually *faire le pont*, 'make a bridge,' by taking off the day in between that and the weekend . . . and naturally nobody works between Christmas and the Réveillon. Plus, a lot of people are starting to observe Valentine's Day in February. Then we all leave town in August for the *vacances*, so Paris more or less shuts down, particularly after the fifteenth . . ."

By now she'd run out of fingers but not holidays. "Then there's school holidays, of course. They take up fourteen weeks of the year, so most parents try to get away for at least some of those."

"Naturally." (Did *anyone* work in this country?)

"As for the skiing season . . . well, it isn't a holiday, of course, but you might think it is from the number of offices that close. The same with hunting. Once the season opens in the middle of September, anyone who owns some land is out with a gun."

Remembering I was in show business gave her more ideas. "And don't forget Cannes in May. It's not official, but for those two weeks of the film festival you won't find a journalist or actor or filmmaker in Paris. The same with the Avignon festival in July. Theater people never miss it. That's where regional theaters choose their shows for the rest of the year . . . And don't forget Fashion Week . . . and the Month of Photography . . . and the FIAC art fair . . ."

"Enough!" Just listening to this recital made me tired.

I'd already learned some other oddities of the French calendar from experience. Museums close on Tuesdays, and on Wednesdays schools hold classes only in the morning. Food and produce markets take Sundays and Mondays off, in return for opening on Saturdays. Even then, many close at 12:30 p.m. and don't reopen until 4 p.m., but then remain open until 8 p.m. Also, for no particular reason that I could discover, our local baker closed on Wednesdays.

And somewhere behind all this, Foucault's pendulum kept its steady tick tick tick, measuring out the hours to a timetable that only Parisians know.

13

SOMETHING TO KILL

The theater Comédie-Italienne, July 19, 1777. The premiere performance of Ernestine, *a new opera by the Chevalier de Saint-Georges, libretto by Choderlos de Laclos, in the presence of the queen. Midway through the first act, a minor character, a coachman, cracks his whip and shouts, "Ohé! Ohé!" This amuses Marie Antoinette. The next time he appears, she calls out, "Ohé!" The courtiers join in. Soon they are calling "Ohé!" at every opportunity. The performance ends in chaos.* Ernestine *won't be performed again for more than a century.*

On the afternoon of July 14, 1789, as his subjects stormed the Bastille prison, igniting the revolution, Louis XVI, twenty-five kilometers away in the palace at Versailles and ignorant of the events that would send him, his family, and most of France's leisure class to the guillotine, updated his diary, summarizing the day in a single word—"Rien" (nothing).

To be fair to Louis, "nothing" didn't mean the day was without incident but rather that he had not gone hunting, and had therefore killed no animals. Among people for whom it was a point of pride to do no work at all and pursue only pleasure, hunting was one of the few activities in which the nobility could honorably indulge. Louis did little else, except work with the court locksmith in tinkering together new and more complicated gadgets. Exasperated, his Austrian wife, Marie Antoinette, complained, "My tastes are not those of the king, who has none, except for hunting and mechanic's labor."

While medieval hunters appreciated the taste of game, the primary function of the chase was sport. The quarry, in particular foxes, wolves, and bears, were chosen as much for their cunning and speed as for culinary possibilities: Oscar Wilde mocked foxhunting as "the unspeakable in pursuit of the uneatable."

When the hunting season ended, the courts reconvened, and young women from good families, known as *débutantes*, or "beginners," were "presented" to the king. Between December and April, in the capitals and fashionable resorts of Europe, hostesses staged parties, balls, and receptions to show off the new crop of marriageable young men and women. Families from the Americas sent their daughters to Europe to be "finished," then, ideally, presented at court, after which they were "out" and regarded as fit to participate in society. Britain's premium such event, Queen Charlotte's Ball, at which four hundred young women were presented at Buckingham Palace each year, was discontinued only in 1958.

For many girls, "coming out" was the first step in snaring a title. They were coached and managed by older and more experienced chaperones—sexual gamekeepers who understood the rules of the social hunt. In recognition of the fact that trapping a titled husband was as much a business as any pursuit in the wild, women who crossed the Atlantic with marriage in mind were known collectively as "the fishing fleet," while the round of balls and receptions at which the hunt took place was called, naturally, "the Season."

✳ · 14 · ✳

STARTING OVER

*Near Fredericksburg, Virginia. May 1975. 4 p.m.
18°C. The floor-to-ceiling shutters of the antebellum
mansion, folded back, trap every breath of air off the
slow-flowing Rappahannock and channel them across
the porch, where we sit sweating and sipping bourbon.
On the walls, decoratively fanned under glass, are
millions in worthless Confederacy "grayback" dollars.
"Gone with the wind?" I joke. Not funny, apparently.*

MOST REVOLUTIONS, IN THE RUSH TO "MAKE IT NEW," BEGIN WITH
the easy stuff: a new flag, a new anthem, new faces on the currency.
The French adopted the blue, white, and red tricolor, embraced the
Marseillaise, and in 1794 replaced the livre and louis d'or (gold louis)
with the franc, streamlined in accordance with the Revolution's most
successful innovation, decimalization.

The revolution's achievements were remarkable. It's been called
the most important single event of the modern era. For the first time
in history, ordinary people seized control of their lives and their

society. They overhauled the legal and educational systems, created academies of science and arts, began the process of eradicating slavery, decriminalized prostitution and homosexuality, and paved the way for full suffrage.

They also established the first scientifically based system of weights and measures, introducing the kilogram and replacing the yard and foot (the latter supposedly based on the length of the foot of Hercules) with the meter, corresponding to a proportion of the circumference of the earth.

Reformers everywhere welcomed the events of 1789. The British poet William Wordsworth could barely contain himself:

> *Bliss was it in that dawn to be alive,*
> *But to be young was very heaven!—Oh! times,*
> *In which the meager, stale, forbidding ways*
> *Of custom, law, and statute, took at once*
> *The attraction of a country in romance!*

The euphoria didn't last. By the time he published that poem in 1809, it bore the rueful title "The French Revolution as It Appeared to Enthusiasts at Its Commencement." Nobody had foreseen the factional fighting that would end with the mass murder of France's intellectual elite and large parts of the privileged classes, including the royal family.

Charles Dickens, writing half a century later in *A Tale of Two Cities*, articulated a general ambivalence about the revolution:

It was the best of times, it was the worst of times, it was the age of wisdom, it was the age of foolishness, it was the epoch of belief, it was the epoch of incredulity, it was the season of Light, it was the season of Darkness, it was the spring of hope, it was the winter of despair, we had everything before us, we had nothing before us, we were all going direct to Heaven, we were all going direct the other way.

For good or ill, France exported its revolution to the world. The American Civil War and the Russian Revolution, which hailed Robespierre as a pioneer Bolshevik, both existed in its shadow. Because of its gory conclusion, however, modern France plays it down. The anniversary of the storming of the Bastille remains the national day, the tricolor its flag, and the Marseillaise its anthem. Until it was replaced by the euro, the franc remained its currency; most of the revolution's advances in science, law, and education survived as well. But like the 1940 surrender to Germany and subsequent occupation, the episode itself is one France prefers to forget.

The Bastille exists today only as an outline embedded in the paving of a busy traffic roundabout and a few stones in the metro station below. There are no individual markers for the thousands of the guillotined buried in such quiet places as the gardens of a convent in Picpus, where they are guarded by the spirit of the Marquis de Lafayette, interred nearby. An exaggeratedly heroic statue of Georges Danton stands at the foot of our street, rue de l'Odéon, marking the former home of the man who was first a friend of

In a contemporary caricature, Robespierre drinks blood squeezed from human hearts.

P. Dien. imp. r. Hautefeuille 32. Paris.

Maximilien de Robespierre, then his victim; but it's the exception. Unless you count a suburban metro station, Robespierre has no monument. "Of all the names of the Terror," said one historian, "no other has remained so execrable in the public memory."

Another furtive survival of that time lies just a few steps across the boulevard from Danton's statue, in a cobbled alley called Cour du Commerce Saint-André. A plaque marks the former home of Tobias Schmidt, a manufacturer of harpsichords who found fortune and dubious fame as the designer and manufacturer of the guillotine. Set high on the outside wall of a restaurant, the plaque is virtually unreadable, presumably not by accident.

Even Napoléon Bonaparte, who rebuilt the shattered nation, isn't as popular as one might expect. No hit musical celebrates his achievements, and the tourists queuing at his grandiloquent tomb behind the Hôtel des Invalides are far outnumbered by the thousands who line up in all weather to descend into the boneyard known as the Catacombs.

Paradoxically, it's the Bourbon kings whom tourists find most seductive. They see in their vulgarity the Kardashians writ large. By the busload, tourists flood the palace of Versailles and its grounds, even more so since the current president took to using it as a stage for meetings with foreign heads of state. Since Charles de Gaulle, French presidents have carried themselves less like civil servants than like kings. Even now, in some quiet corner of France's presidential palace, the Élysée, a flunky may be dusting off a throne as the tailor runs up some twenty-first-century imperial robes.

❊ · 15 · ❊

THE NEW ERA

Paris. May 1770. Austrian princess Marie Antoinette, fourteen years old, arrives in Paris to marry sixteen-year-old Louis XVI, future king of France. As she's driven through the city, students of the Collège Louis-le-Grand wait in the rain to cheer. One of their brightest, twelve-year-old Maximilien de Robespierre, reads a poem of welcome he's written. Twenty-three years later, he will sign the warrant that sends her to the guillotine.

GIVEN THE IMPORTANCE TO THE FRENCH OF WEATHER AND THE seasons, it was natural that the revolutionaries of 1789 should set about remaking them in the image of the new France.

As a first step, they reset the date. The year 1792 became Year I. A medal struck for the occasion spelled out the precise instant: *"L'ère des Français commencé à l'équinoxe d'automne 22 Sept. 1792, 9 heures 19 min. 50 s. du matin à Paris"* (The French era began at the autumnal equinox, September 22, 1792, at 9:19:50 a.m. Paris time).

Revising a calendar authorized by Julius Caesar in 46 BCE and last updated by Pope Gregory XIII in 1582 was a bigger job than France's new masters imagined. Centuries of use had cemented it deep in the daily life of Christian Europe. To undermine its foundations threatened the entire edifice.

But not to change it would compromise everything for which the revolution was fought. In the words of the man whose name became synonymous with the new calendar, "The regeneration of the French people and the establishment of the Republic entailed the reform of all that came before. It was as if we had not lived at all during those years spent under the oppression of kings. The prejudices of the throne and the church poisoned every page of the ancient calendar."

As a first step, a nine-man commission was convened to explore options. It included the astronomers and mathematicians Joseph-Louis Lagrange, Joseph Jérôme Lefrançois de Lalande, Gaspard Monge, and Alexandre Guy Pingré. Chemist Louis-Bernard Guyton de Morveau, another member, was not an obvious choice, although he had helped create the first systematic catalog of minerals, so he might at least know where to begin.

Almost as important as the scientific expertise of these men was their political reliability. Nobody should be too identifiable with the ancien régime. They didn't come more solid than Lagrange. Italian by birth, he believed that "one of the first principles of every wise man is to conform strictly to the laws of the country in which he is living, even when they are unreasonable." Nor was one likely to hear a discouraging word from Charles-Gilbert Romme, the commission's chairman. Described as "a small, awkward and clumsy man with an ill complexion, and a dull orator," he could be relied on to deliver the conclusions desired by whoever was in power at the time.

Hindsight shows that these gentlemen, however distinguished in their own fields, weren't particularly qualified for their task. But who would be? It was one nobody had seriously undertaken for centuries. Revising the calendar required someone with a fresh viewpoint, uncluttered by scholarship or reverence for history.

As is often the case, the moment produced the man. The person who would do most of the work in creating the new calendar and bear the burden of responsibility was the youngest, least educated, and most obscure of the commission's members: Philippe-François-Nazaire Fabre, better known as Fabre d'Églantine, or Fabre of the Wild Rose.

If the term "loose cannon" had existed in the 1780s, it would have been applied to Fabre. Poet, actor, singer, and playwright, he was, at forty, younger than his colleagues on the commission by at least a decade and, in their eyes, insultingly unqualified.

A single but crucial distinction fitted him for the post: he had friends in high places. Specifically, he was a protégé of Georges Danton, the spellbinding orator who, along with the ascetic Maximilien de Robespierre, dominated the new state.

Brutish in looks and build, Danton compensated for his pockmarked face, further scarred by a childhood encounter with a bull,

Georges Danton.

by exercising his flair for the dramatic and his mesmerizing baritone voice. In his distinctive red surcoat, he was the undisputed king of the Mountain, as members of the Convention—the elected body in charge of the country, its congress—called the high-banked seating of the Chambre des Députés.

In Fabre, Danton recognized someone with his own hunger for the limelight. He was a dangerous patron, with many enemies, but neither man was a stranger to taking chances. As Danton urged in one of his most famous speeches, "Boldness, more boldness, always boldness!"

Under a monarchy, no person as lowborn as Fabre or Danton could have achieved high office or taken part in national politics. But during the revolution, an ability to rouse the mob and win its support meant more than position or fortune. Oratory launched reputations. "Public diction," says historian Simon Schama in his book *Citizens*, "was public power."

As politicians visited the theater to pick up points of technique, performers became celebrities overnight. It took Fabre, a newcomer from the south, only two years to become one of the city's most popular playwrights. A tragedy, *Augusta*, failed, but he had a hit in 1790 with *Le Philinte de Molière, ou La suite du Misanthrope* (Molière's Philinte, or the sequel to *The Misanthrope*), a parody of Molière's famous play. Audiences intimidated by the original enjoyed his easily digested parody.

His colorful name inevitably attracted attention. He explained that he'd added the "Églantine" himself in honor of the golden rose

Fabre d'Églantine with his fictional golden rose.

presented to him by none other than Clémence Isaure herself, doyenne of Toulouse's Acadèmia dels Jòcs Florals, or Academy of the Floral Games, for the public recitation of an original poetic work, in his case a sonnet dedicated to the Virgin Mary.

At forty, Fabre was older than the leading figures of the revolution. But "Fabre d'Églantine" was a role like any other, with a costume to go with it, and he was above all an actor. Abandoning powdered wigs and brocaded surcoats for open-necked shirts, he let his hair grow and wore it swept back from his high forehead, with a prominent widow's peak. Instead of satin breeches that ended at the knee, he adopted the simple cotton trousers of the common people that earned them the name *les sans-culottes*—those without pants.

His glib self-promotion didn't fool everyone, least of all his patron. "Danton liked his wit," says Simon Schama, "and pretended to like his plays, but he was under no illusions about Fabre's virtue." Robespierre, nicknamed "the Incorruptible," dismissed him as a man "of principles but no virtue; talents but no soul; skillful in the art of depicting men, much more skillful in deceiving them."

Backed by Danton, Fabre became president of the Cordeliers Club, named for the group that had met in the chapel of the Franciscan monks to plot revolution. It was from its pulpit that Danton first made his reputation as a public speaker. Fabre was elected to the Convention in 1792 and served as a deputy for two years, voting with Danton in most things, including for the execution of Louis XVI. When Danton became minister of justice, Fabre, along with Danton's old friend Camille Desmoulins, was appointed his private secretary, responsible for writing some of his speeches.

And once a commission was convened to debate the new calendar, who better to keep an eye on its deliberations than the ambitious Fabre?

16

ON THE BEACH

*Lady Jane Beach, Sydney, Australia. November 1986.
2 p.m. 18°C. Steps hewn from the sandstone zigzag
down to a crescent of yellow sand. Nude men, oiled,
tanned, and lithe, sun themselves on the stair-side terraces, as flagrantly on offer as meat on a butcher's slab.
At the water's edge, ankle deep in waves that barely rise
above a languid ripple, a young couple wades naked,
hand in hand, she heavy-breasted and wide-hipped, he
spectacularly well-hung.*

"MOTHER'S JUST HAD A *THALASSOTHÉRAPIE*," MARIE-DOMINIQUE
said. "It did her a lot of good. Maybe I should have one." She turned
sideways and looked at herself critically in the mirror. "What do you
think?"

"I have no idea what you're talking about," I said. "A thalawhat?"

"*Thalassothérapie.* Doesn't that exist in Australia?"

"Search me. What is it?"

"A sort of health treatment using products of the sea. You know, *thalassa*—Greek for 'sea'? Imagine a health farm or a spa, but with seawater."

"Then it's not for me. Remember—I can't swim."

"Doesn't matter. There's no swimming involved."

"How can there be . . . ? "

But I knew it was pointless to ask. This was all about *maman*. If her mother was looking good, Marie-Dominique wouldn't be satisfied until she'd had the same treatment.

By March and April, long gone are the holidays but not the flab, nor those accumulated toxins that cause one to regard a slice of foie gras with less appetite than revulsion. And one can already see the summer looming, and the months of July and August, when one's body is exposed to the often unkind attention of neighbors and friends.

In the Middle Ages, these were the months when people set out on pilgrimages to the holy places of Christendom. Today they still travel, though the regeneration they seek is less spiritual than physical. Modern pilgrims don't head for Chartres or Santiago de Compostela but to Dinard or Île de Ré, more intent on purging their bodies than cleansing their souls.

Two weeks later, we stood on the deck of a ferry and watched the low outline of Île de Ré emerge from the sea mist. A new road bridge linked this offshore island to the mainland, transforming a sleepy backwater into one of the most fashionable hideaways along the Atlantic coast. Until the bridge, it had harbored a few beach-combers and locals involved in the oyster trade. Now they were

outnumbered by city people in search of better health through thalassotherapy.

A minibus carried us across to the ocean side, where a score of
six-story Edwardian mansions lined the beach, a fragment of Paris's
sixteenth arrondissement transported to the Charente coast. Once
the summer retreats of Paris's wealthy, they now served as guest-
houses for clients of the nearby clinics.

Six thousand kilometers to the west, on the same latitude, almost
identical houses—disingenuously called "cottages" by their million-
aire owners—lined the shores of Rhode Island and Martha's Vineyard. Yet as far as I'd been able to discover, no American resorts
offered thalassotherapy. Only the British shared the French belief
that seawater, both inside and outside the body, was conducive to
good health.

Even more puzzling, the therapy only worked with the cooler
waters of the Atlantic. Clinics fringed the western coast and the
French side of the English Channel, but none existed on the Mediterranean. If there was any therapeutic value in their climate, it resided
in the sun alone.

The low, modern building on Île de Ré to which the bus delivered us made no concessions to comfort or style. Behind its picture
windows, figures in white shuffled lethargically or sprawled on daybeds, staring out to sea. I looked for a sign over the door warning
"Abandon Foie Gras, Côte de Boeuf, and Châteauneuf-du-Pape,
All Ye Who Enter Here."

Unceremoniously registered, we were sent to separate changing rooms. I was relieved of everything but swimming trunks and issued with a robe and flip-flops. Nobody explained the treatment I was to receive. French doctors, I'd learned from experience, didn't recognize the term "bedside manner." Putting patients at their ease rated somewhere below choosing new curtains for the waiting room.

When I came out, Marie-Dominique was nowhere in sight.

"Where's madame?" I asked.

"Treatments for men and women are separate," said a receptionist. "Madame will meet you at the main pool afterward." She pointed down a long corridor. "Room seventeen."

Feeling ambushed, I followed her directions, the flip-flops dictating that somnambulistic shamble I'd noticed in other clients. Each unmarked door I passed brought to mind the shenanigans described by Michel Houellebecq in his novels *The Elementary Particles* and *Platform*.

A cynic beside whom even Jean-Paul Sartre appeared sunny, Houellebecq saw only corruption and decadence in France's health resorts, spas, nudist beaches, and *thalassa* clinics. Most, he suggested, were nothing but pickup spots where the young and hard-bodied, in return for favors or money, made themselves available to the old, flabby, and rich.

In his novel *Platform*, the main character and his girlfriend, exhausted by a trawl through the fleshpots of Asia, sign up for a recuperative thalassotherapy in a resort along the channel coast, but find no escape from the tyranny of the daily, if not hourly, orgasm.

Some readers, hoping he wrote from experience, had been

disappointed to find that actual thalassotherapy was much less fun. "Before I started reading [*Platform*]," wrote British novelist Julian Barnes, "a friend gave me an unexpected warning: 'There's a scene where the narrator and his girlfriend and another woman have a threesome in the hammam [steam room] at the thalassotherapy center in Dinard.' His tone hardening, he went on, 'Well, I've been there, and it's *just not possible*.'"

Was good health the only thing on offer? I kept my eyes and ears open as a helper led me to my first appointment. But if moans of ecstasy were being generated, not a whisper of them escaped through these featureless doors.

Room seventeen was plain, white, narrow, about the width of a railway carriage but half the length. Just inside, a woman in a white coat with arms like hams stood behind a counter. My mind flashed back alarmingly to a sauna I'd visited in Finland. Similar ladies, wearing floor-length plastic aprons, had grabbed me as I emerged, reeling with heat, thrown me facedown on a table, and scraped me almost raw with the sort of brushes normally used to scrub floors.

This lady motioned for me to remove my robe and walk to the far end of the room.

"*Attention!*" she ordered. (Watch out!)

As I turned to face her, a stream of water slammed me against the wall with fire-hose force. What I'd taken for a counter actually enclosed a kind of hydrant, with a heavy-duty canvas hose and a brass nozzle attached. Mouth and nose filled with seawater, I tried to fend off the stream. No hope. For three minutes, every inch of my body was battered by the torrent. If you could drown standing up, this was the way to do it.

When it ended I let myself be led, reeling, ears ringing, half-conscious, into another room. In the center sat a galvanized tank the size of a dumpster. Shakily, I ascended a set of steel steps and, too numb to resist, sank into the warm water. It was just about neck deep, but by grabbing straps attached to the edge of the tank I could keep my head above the surface.

Somewhere out of sight, a motor started up and the water began to churn. At the same time, an attendant decanted a coffee can full of ashlike powder into the bath.

"Hey! What's that?"

She shrugged. "L'algue, m'sieur."

Seaweed? Buoyed up by the roiling water, I watched the powder dissolve. It left behind an odor both medicinal and culinary, somewhere between bronchial inhalation and chicken broth. The sensation wasn't unpleasant. I began to drowse. Did they add some special ingredients to the seaweed soup? A spoonful or two of cannabis, or a little hashish?

After an indeterminate time someone helped me out of the bath and led me into a shower, where I washed off the slightly slimy residue of my immersion. Just as I finished, a second door opened and a pretty woman looked in. Her short white coat didn't look the least bit medical.

"Nous sommes prêts, m'sieur?"

Was I ready? What for? Beyond her, I saw a small room unfurnished except for a thin mattress on the floor. Was I to be offered, in best Houellebecqian fashion, what the massage trade termed a "happy ending"?

In fact, what I received was a decidedly unerotic and probably therapeutic rubdown from the young masseuse, who obviously knew her job. As she worked, we chatted. She had actually been to Australia and had happy memories of, among other places, Bendigo. I let my mind roam the wide streets of this entirely unexceptional Victorian country town. Nothing could have been more calming, or less erotic.

On slightly wobbly legs, I joined Marie-Dominique on one of the daybeds in the solarium.

"So how was it?" she asked.

"Oh, you know. Relaxing."

"I thought you'd enjoy it," she said.

I wasn't sure that "enjoy" was the mot juste. And nothing I'd experienced compared with the pleasures described by Houellebecq. But I'd entered only a few of the clinic's many rooms. Perhaps, as in life, it was a question of knowing on which doors to knock.

17

ENTER FABRE, PURSUED BY A BEAR

Jardin du Luxembourg, Paris 6me. February 1996.
2°C. The air hushed and still with the promise of snow.
Beginning above Montparnasse and rolling downhill
in a wave, all color bleeds out of the landscape, antic-
ipating by a few seconds the white flakes soon sifting
down, turning what had been pastel Monet to a mono-
chrome Brassaï.

Being an actor or actress at the end of the eighteenth century was not what every mother would wish for her child.

Owning money or land was the only serious test of a person's worth. They signified that the owner need do nothing in life but enjoy it. For those forced to work, there were the professions: medicine, law, the army or navy, the church—followed by the last, worst choice, trade: making and selling things. After that, nothing much remained but crime and show business. People didn't take up the stage so much as descend to it.

Philippe Fabre was born in 1750 in Carcassonne, in the far south. His father, a wool merchant, worked for his wife's father and hated it, a resentment he took out on his son, the only child of six to survive to adulthood. "I was raised by a father who detested me and a mother I detested," Philippe wrote.

Local schools educated boys only to age twelve, after which they were deemed old enough to work. (Women were seldom educated at all. Their mothers taught them to cook and sew.) Promising male students continued their studies in church schools. Philippe was sent to the Jesuits in nearby Limoux. From its priests, the church's intellectual elite, he learned to speak Greek and Latin, to draw and write. Since he possessed an exceptional voice, with a range from bass to countertenor, they also taught him to read music and sing.

At twenty Fabre was tall for the time, with a mass of brown hair and a face unmarked by the smallpox that scarred so many. Unlikely to flourish in either the wool trade or the priesthood, he was saved from having to choose by the arrival in Limoux of a traveling theater troupe. He left with it.

Wandering companies under an actor/manager were a feature of life in Europe. Marlowe and Molière learned their trade on the road; as did Shakespeare, who put such a company into *Hamlet*. But people of their talent were the exception. Most troupes, grumbled one magistrate, were "little better than traveling brothels." He didn't exaggerate. "Actress" was synonymous with "prostitute," and the average actor was a rootless vagabond who strutted in ragged costumes, clowning and declaiming as he debated whether to pick your pocket or ravish your wife.

Fabre soon made himself useful. His voice and musical skill helped in writing and performing the one-act playlets with music known as "operas," and he could dash off rhyming verse almost to order. Perhaps it wasn't top quality, but a road company wasn't the Comédie-Française.

He also upheld the profession's reputation for bad behavior with women. "A good talker," conceded a colleague, before observing sourly that "his seductions were conducted with a certain brutality."

A letter to Fabre from a woman named Sophie Proudhon, dated September 29, 1776, has survived. "My dear friend," she wrote, "how happy I am. I could die of joy. What a charming letter, to tell me that before the Feast of Saint John, my friend, my tender friend, will be with me. How I will count the hours."

If Sophie hoped to marry her "dear friend," she was out of luck. So were Jeanette in Grenoble, Marie in Versailles, an anonymous brunette in Bordeaux, and a blonde in Troyes. Fabre jilted them all in favor of his latest conquest, Catherine Desremond, known affectionately as Catiche.

The attraction of Catiche was that of forbidden fruit. Only fifteen, she was the daughter of the couple who managed the troupe. The more her parents discouraged it, the stronger the attachment became, until in 1777 when the company was playing at Namur, Belgium, under the patronage of the local archbishop, they eloped.

The constabulary caught them and brought them back. Fabre,

who had deflowered Catiche and, what was worse, tried to deprive her parents of her services as an actress, was charged with theft and condemned to hang. His fellow performers appealed for clemency, and the conviction was reduced to lifetime banishment from Belgium.

Fleeing back to his native south, Fabre didn't show his face in the north until 1787. That year, now styling himself Philippe Fabre d'Églantine, with a florid new signature to go with it, he turned up in Paris with a wife, the actress Marie Nicole Godin-Lesage, and a valise full of unperformed plays. Having flirted in the meantime with running his own theatrical troupe and also managing a couple of regional theaters, he was heavily in debt.

News traveled slowly in those days, so details of his past took some time to catch up with him. They may have arrived with the soldiers of the south who made their way from Marseilles to join the revolution in 1789.

In peacetime, these rural clods would not have voyaged any farther than the next village, but a pike and a uniform of sorts—sometimes no more than a blue, white, and red cockade or sash—could carry you a long way. As they marched, they sang a belligerent new song that its composer, Rouget de Lisle, named "La Marseillaise" in their honor. It would be adopted in 1795 as the anthem of the new French state.

Someone in these new arrivals may have recognized Fabre and confided over a bottle of wine that the former actor was a fraud. In coming to Paris, he was fleeing from a mountain of debt, not to mention numerous jilted young women. As for winning the golden rose at Toulouse, he had in fact received only second prize, the silver lily. The same men hooted at the claim that Clémence Isaure had presented it. Clémence Isaure didn't exist. She was a character created to personify the festival—a synthetic figure, like Marianne, the symbol of the revolution.

If anyone confronted him with his lies, Fabre probably argued that lilies were the emblem of the disgraced Bourbon monarchy and therefore to be shunned. Also, "Fabre d'Églantine" had a nicer ring. The debts and the women he just shrugged off. He could afford to do so, since he had become one of the overnight sensations of prerevolutionary Paris.

He owed his new reputation to a song for which he wrote the words. "Il pleut, bergère" (It's raining, shepherdess) appeared in a one-act comic opera, *Laure et Pétrarque*, written in 1780, with music by Louis-Victor Simon. The show flopped, but the tune flourished. It was even taken up as a marching song by the National Guard, the revolutionary force that replaced the royalist army, and it is still sung by schoolchildren more than two centuries later.

Anyone raised in a rural society would have recognized the story told by the song.

> Il pleut, il pleut, bergère
> Rentre tes blancs moutons
> Allons sous ma chaumière
> Bergère, vite allons.

J'entends sous le feuillage.
L'eau qui tombe à grand bruit.
Voici, venir l'orage.
Voici l'éclair qui luit.

(It's raining, shepherdess. / Round up your white sheep. / Shelter in my cottage. / Shepherdess, come quickly. / I'm waiting under the thatch. / The rain is falling loudly. / See the lightning flash.)

By the sixth verse, the singer has maneuvered the shepherdess into bed with the promise that once the storm subsides, he will ask her father for her hand in marriage.

If one didn't have to sit outside in all weathers, constantly rounding up the flock, fending off predators, and extricating the animals from bogs and thornbushes, the life of a shepherdess might seem idyllic. Marie Antoinette, at least, thought so. In the Hameau de la Reine, a stylized village on the grounds of Versailles, she and her ladies played at being peasants, grooming animals chosen for their pulchritude and milking cows into pails of porcelain made to order at the Sèvres factory.

Marie Antoinette must have heard "Il pleut, bergère" and may have taken the song as a kind of tribute. This would help explain why, on February 22, 1789, her husband, the king, signed a surprising document that, literally at the stroke of a pen, made Fabre's financial problems disappear. It read, "His Majesty, wishing to give to 'sieur Fabre d'Églantine the means to order his affairs, gives him safe conduct for the period of six months, during which His Majesty forbids his creditors to exercise any claims against him; likewise also all bailiffs and sergeants to arrest or trouble him." By the time this amnesty ran out, the revolution had begun, and with it a new way of life for Fabre.

18

SAYING LESS, MEANING MORE

Hot night. Lightning flares.
Gasp of wind. Thunder cracks.
Downpour. Ah, so cool!

IF YOU WANT A WINDY PARIS, MARCH IS YOUR MONTH. BRISK breezes sweep away those clouds that build up on February afternoons and furnish the gaudy sunsets beloved of Rubens. By contrast, April's pale, cloudless skies look as well scrubbed as a Vermeer.

Rounding the corner onto avenue Winston Churchill, I was buffeted by an eddy of air solid as a shoulder. Big buildings created wind tunnels, and this corner of the right bank had two of the largest.

The block-long Grand Palais, or Great Palace, sufficiently long and high to house a 767, stands as grandiose as a moored ocean liner in the heart of the right bank. Its domed glass roof makes it the preferred setting for blockbuster art shows and displays of everything from equitation to farm machinery.

Across the street, the Petit Palais, or Little Palace, tries but fails not to be upstaged. Neither building was ever a palace. Dating from the late nineteenth century, they were built to house the expositions at which France boasted its expertise in industry, design, and art—in the case of the Petit Palais, the Universal Exposition of 1900. Once the fashion for such displays of excess declined, the Petit Palais became the City of Paris Fine Arts Museum, a cousin to the national collection housed in the former Gare d'Orsay railway terminal, just visible on the other side of the Seine.

Statuary groups of writhing naked figures populated the building's exterior, making the ancient world look more exciting than it had been in real life. Admirers of excess found the result enchanting. One was Leopold II of Belgium, the tyrant of the Belgian Congo who, in the process of looting its natural resources, killed more than ten million of its inhabitants. The Petit Palais so impressed him that he kept its architect in work for decades. (Not surprisingly, Leopold isn't mentioned on the palace's website.)

The website is, in fact, notably short on detail, which was why on entering the museum's entry hall I headed for a uniformed guard, a rare speck of humanity in a cavern of murals and white marble.

"Je cherche *Le Vent*," I told him.

He peered at me as if I had uttered some obscure African war cry. "*Comment?*"

"Er . . . *Le Vent?*"

I gave the pronunciation my best shot, complete with an attempt at the *moue*, that disposition of the mouth in which one pushes out the lower lip and presses the upper lip against the teeth to produce the "eeuw" sound without which certain French words make no sense.

Judging by the blank look on the face of the *gardien*, I didn't succeed. All those hours watching Maurice Chevalier movies, wasted.

Maybe I had the name wrong. If the work I was looking for wasn't called *The Wind*, perhaps it was *The Storm*.

"*L'Orage?*" I suggested.

Inside the blue serge uniform, his shoulders began to assume that configuration, as characteristic as the *moue*, that we call a shrug. The French know it as *un haussement d'épaules*, a term that, like "passing gas," describes an act but omits any suggestion of its significance. If you press a Frenchman to be more precise, the best you'll get is another shrug.

From behind me a man said quietly in English, "Perhaps I can help."

My savior was, unexpectedly, Japanese. He looked to be about my age, gray haired, bespectacled, and dressed in a dark suit.

He spoke in rapid French to the guard, who responded with equal speed. The former embodiment of ignorance became a fount of information.

"I believe the figure you're looking for," said the Japanese gentleman, once he had finished, "is *Tempête et ses nuées* by François-Raoul Larche."

His *moue* on "nuées" was faultless. If one doesn't understand a language, the next best thing is to pronounce it well. I put this belief into practice immediately.

"*Arigatou gozaimasu*," I said and bowed.

"*Douitashimashite.*" He followed his responding bow with a torrent of Japanese, which I halted by holding up my hand, palm out, like a traffic cop.

"Sorry," I said. "But that's almost the only phrase I know. Except . . ." I took a breath. ". . . *Onako ga suite imasu.*"

"Ah, yes." He nodded. "Very good. But perhaps you mean *Onoka ga suite imasu,* 'I am hungry,' yes?"

"Forgive my pronunciation. I've only visited Japan a few times."

"No, your accent is excellent," he lied diplomatically. "But by all means, let us continue in English." He held out his hand. "Yamada Minosuke. So you are interested in *Tempête et ses nuées?*"

"If it's the piece I'm thinking of," I said. "I've only seen photographs. Is it a statue, or rather a sculpture, of a storm, represented by a female . . ."

I stopped myself from miming her pose. One look at my impression of a naked woman, eyes wide, arms spread, mouth howling as she flung herself out of a sort of bronze waterspout, and the guard would have thrown me down the front steps.

Fortunately I didn't need to. "I know this piece," Minosuke said. "The title translates as 'storm and its clouds.' I believe it's in the permanent collection. Shall we see if we can find it?"

He led me confidently up the curving marble staircase.

"You must come here a lot," I said. "Are you an art historian?"

He sighed. "No. Sadly, excuse me. I am a tour guide. I often bring groups here."

Tempête et ses nuées *by François-Raoul Larche.*

I didn't volunteer that I too dabbled in the dark art of the guided tour. Instead, I told him why the sculpture interested me. He was immediately intrigued.

"In Japan, we are also most interested in the weather. It has inspired some of our greatest poetry."

"Oh, you mean haiku?"

The five-seven-five syllable pattern of these little poems seldom adapts perfectly to other languages, but experimenting with it can be as absorbing as completing the *Times* crossword puzzle.

Traditionally, a haiku refers to something in nature. The springtime cherry blossoms in Tokyo's Ueno Park and the crowds who walk there, intoxicated by the pink storm, have inspired thousands. I quoted one of the most famous:

> *"Wind through cherry trees*
> *Fragile petals shaken loose*
> *Drifting like pink snow."*

Minosuke pursed his lips. "Yes ... not *quite* like the great Bashō. But most interesting. Do you know ...

> *"Hatsu shigure*
> *Sarumo komino o*
> *hoshido nari*

"In English, you might say:

> *"The first cold shower.*
> *Even the monkey seems to want*
> *A little coat of straw."*

"That's not the version I know," I said, "but there's another:

> *"Winter downpour;*
> *Even the monkey*
> *Needs a raincoat."*

Minosuke actually giggled. "Oh, yes. This is most clever. Speaking of haiku and rain . . ."

I didn't get to see *Tempête et ses nuées*, at least not that day. Instead, we sat in the Palais café for an hour, emptying pot after pot of tea and talking haiku, or rather, as my new friend corrected me, its plural, *haïkaï*.

In doing so, we reaffirmed an affinity between France and Japan, between literature and art, but, above all, between art and the seasons. Those roots were old and deep. Japanese ukiyo-e woodblock prints inspired the impressionists, in particular Claude Monet. The exercises in word and image Guillaume Apollinaire called "calligrammes" were a union of calligraphy and the haiku. *Sept haïkaï* is a signature work of the composer Olivier Messiaen.

As the philosopher Heraclitus said in Hellenic Greek, "Panta rhei": all things flow. And they often flow through Paris.

19

TALL POPPIES

*Rue de l'Odéon, Paris 6me. December 2017. 10 a.m.
3°C. The doorbell rings in midmorning. It's our post-
lady with a sheaf of card-bound almanacs, one of which
we purchase—our Christmas tip in polite disguise. The
almanac includes a calendar, with the saints' names for
each day. Times of sunrise and moonrise. A map of
France; another of our region, Île-de-France; Paris
itself; and the Métro. The printer has shoehorned a few
recipes into leftover space. Next to them, less interesting than baked pork chops and chicken en brochette, is
a cramped map of the European Union.*

DANTON PROBABLY EXPECTED FABRE, HIS SPY ON THE COMMIS-
sion, to do no more than keep his ears open and mouth shut. But he
may not have been entirely surprised when his protégé emerged as
the most vigorous champion of a *Calendrier républicain*.

For someone with political ambitions, it was a dream project.
The Gregorian calendar, conceived by a tyrant and modified by a
pope, embodied everything the revolution abhorred. The man who

substituted a republican alternative could expect the gratitude of the nation.

The other members of the commission were not about to provoke someone as well-connected as Fabre. They decided to let him wear himself out. When he got bored and lost interest, his elders and betters could step in. Until then, they followed the instincts of generations of seat warmers and time servers, sending their apologies to most meetings and only turning up with sufficient frequency to justify their stipend. By default, Fabre was left in charge.

Fabre had never held office, nor did his history suggest a fitness to do so. But knowledge and experience no longer counted. Paradoxically, ignorance was a survival characteristic. Egalitarian cultures often cut down to size those who dare lift their heads above the mob. In revolutionary France, the so-called tall poppy syndrome applied literally. Thousands of scholars and intellectuals would die on the guillotine for no better reason than that they knew more than the *sans-culottes*, and showed it.

The theatrical flair with which Fabre approached the calendar project was typical. Sketching the parameters in broad strokes, he left others to fill in the gaps. Once they were done, he reemerged to become its public face. Any pronouncements or updates to the Convention were done by him.

Some key decisions had already been made. It went without saying that any updated calendar must incorporate that avatar of republican France, the metric system, based on multiples of the number ten. As a first step, Fabre lengthened the hour from sixty to a hundred minutes. Ten such hours made up a day. As the new day was substantially shorter—1,000 minutes, compared to the old day's 1,440—he extended the week from seven days to ten, called a *décade*, with the tenth a day of rest. Three *décades* made a month, and twelve months of equal length a year.

Since they had their origin in ancient religious rituals, day names also had to go. Monday, Tuesday, and Wednesday became *primidi* (day one), *duodi* (day two), and *tridi* (day three), followed by *quartidi*, *quintidi*, *sextidi*, *septidi*, *octidi*, *nonidi*, and *décadi*.

So far, so straightforward. This part of the scheme wasn't even particularly novel. Others who had tried to rationalize the calendar had suggested similar changes. In 1788, poet, atheist, and anarchist Pierre-Sylvain Maréchal published his *Honest Man's Almanac*, which substituted the names of famous men from history for those of saints. Ahead of his time, Maréchal suffered the full force of the church's disapproval. He was imprisoned for four months and forbidden to ever publish again under his own name.

With the architecture of the new year established, Fabre and his helpers made an even more sweeping change. The Republican year would not commence around the anniversary of Christ's birth but rather with a date more significant for the Frenchman on the land—the end of the harvest. The first day of the year became the former October 6. But for symmetry, and with an eye to symbolism, Fabre backdated it to the autumnal equinox, September 22, one of only two occasions when day and night are equal in length.

Each November, with the grapes and grain gathered in, farmers traditionally laid the dust of the harvest with a wine made from freshly pressed Gamay grapes and matured for just three weeks. They saw no reason to change this custom simply because some fool in Paris was fiddling with the calendar. As they drank their Beaujolais nouveau in the autumn of 1793, the more thoughtful among them might have intuited that the wine, young and fresh but with little character, reflected the nature of the new calendar, if not of the revolution itself.

20

IF WINTER COMES . . .

*Boulevard Saint-Germain. Paris 6me. November. 4°C.
Outside the café Les Deux Magots, a whiff of burning charcoal signifies that the chestnut seller is back at
his old pitch, tending his improvised oil-drum stove. A
dozen nuts smolder and crack on the ash-dusted metal.
He shovels some into a white paper bag, around which a
woman cups her palms: no hand warmer more effective,
nor more fragrant.*

I'D WATCHED THE SEASONS CHANGE ON FOUR CONTINENTS, BUT
never as they did in Paris. As F. Scott Fitzgerald wrote, "Life starts
all over again when it gets crisp in the fall." Along the boulevards,
one could sense the machinery meshing, cogs sliding into place as
the engine of the year rotated into its final quarter.

The change can occur in a few seconds—as long as it takes a
clock to strike the hour—and when one least expects it.

Crossing rue Bonaparte, beyond the tiny stall where a man
cooks crepes to order on the hot plate—another winter smell: that

of burnt sugar and Nutella chocolate-and-hazelnut paste—I spotted a further harbinger.

Yaseen Khan had once again hung his artwork from the railings of the little garden behind the church of Saint-Germain-des-Prés, each smudgy abstract surrounded by text in spiky calligraphy. He's as much a fixture of this corner as the chestnut seller or the crepe man, and I seldom stop to look. But that day I did pause, because he'd chosen texts from a favorite poem, Jacques Prévert's "Les Feuilles mortes" (the dead leaves).

To the corner of each stiff, parchmentlike paper was pinned a dead sycamore leaf. As much for the leaf as the poem I bought one, and, juggling it awkwardly as I fumbled for my ticket, only just managed to catch the 95 bus, direction Porte de Montmartre.

Squeezing into a seat, I adjusted my mental almanac to the passing of a season. The date could not have been more precise or final had it been printed on a calendar. Not savagely, like a wolf, as the Russians see it, but in the French style, silently, secretly, as a rime of ice gathers on still water in the night, winter was upon us.

Walking through the Jardins du Luxembourg an hour before, I'd seen the signs, just not recognized them. Instead, I was distracted by one of the twenty statues of France's great women, larger than life, that surround the formal gardens of Marie de Médicis.

All but one of these statues depict queens or saints. The exception is the figure of a woman who, despite the cross around her neck and the wreath of laurel in her hair, stands in the seductive hipshot pose we associate more with showgirls. Flowers and more laurel

Yaseen Khan, artist of the Paris streets.

leaves line her cloak, suggestive of someone not unacquainted with sensual pleasure. She is Clémence Isaure, the imaginary doyenne of Toulouse from whom Fabre d'Églantine claimed to have received his fictitious golden rose.

Walking on, I didn't notice that the tall date palms that had guarded Le Nôtre's tranquil garden all summer were gone. Overnight, while the gates were shut (the time when everything of importance happens in the most discreet of Paris's parks), forklifts conveyed the trees in their green-painted wooden crates to a graveled space behind the Musée du Luxembourg, creating a transient oasis through which I'd walked without taking notice. By now the trees would be installed inside the lofty hall of the Orangerie, safe from the frosts, which the evergreens that replaced them would just shrug off.

Then there were the leaves. Overnight, gardeners had corralled the fallen chestnut, plane, and sycamore leaves in the millions and heaped them in chicken-wire cages, each large enough to contain an automobile. Those that escaped made a carpet ankle-deep under the trees, or blew onto rue de Médicis to clog its gutters or plaster themselves to the sidewalks in a collage of beiges and browns.

London had just as many deciduous trees as Paris, but I didn't remember seeing leaves in such abundance along the Mall or in Regent's Park. Did their staffs do a better job of raking? I doubted it. Rather, those who maintained the Luxembourg chose to let leaves accumulate. Far from being a problem, they were part of the show.

At the end of my trip across the city, the bus deposited me in Montmartre. Busy, built up, high above Paris to the north, it's a long way from the Luxembourg. As leaves don't lie long in these windy streets, I wasn't expecting to see any, which made what I found in La Souris Verte all the more surprising.

Away from the tourist trails, cafés cease to be a subject of curiosity for visitors and revert to an amenity for the French—somewhere to dawdle over a coffee, read the paper, do business, meet friends, watch *le foot*, and argue about last night's result over a glass of Stella.

La Souris Verte (The Green Mouse) belongs in this category. The skylight over its high back room, the walls of unplastered brick, a

Autumn leaves on the floor of La Souris Verte.

bare-board floor unscrubbed since the de Gaulle administration, and some rugged stools and tables bolted together from balks of squared-off timber and looking suspiciously like recycled workbenches all suggest onetime industrial use—possibly as a sweatshop, a suspicion supported by a few tables adapted from old sewing-machine benches complete with foot treadles incorporating the Singer logo in wrought iron.

Some nights there's a band, but mostly the sound system mumbles music chosen by whomever is behind the bar: thumping techno one day, the next some Belle Epoque art songs by Reynaldo Hahn or the mournful contralto of Nina Simone.

In the corner next to the bar, a stringless guitar and an ancient weighing machine with a broken glass emphasize that this is no *branché* boulevardier hangout. Hence my surprise that afternoon at finding its floor strewn with dead leaves.

Had they blown in? Unlikely. The door was closed, the sidewalk clear, with not a tree in sight.

I raised an eyebrow to the girl polishing glasses behind the bar. She shrugged.

"C'est pour le Beaujolais nouveau."

The last cog meshed in the machinery of the changing season. Others more attuned to the seasons than I had seen the signs and, each in his own way, marked the occasion.

That morning, on rue des Écoles, a café owner had scattered straw across the entrance and placed a bale by the door. It was a reminder of the harvest, but there was also a notice from one of the big wine merchants stuck to his window announcing, "Le Beaujolais nouveau est arrivé" and urging us to sample it.

Nothing signified the shift from autumn to winter so visibly, at least for city people, as the arrival of the new Beaujolais on the third Thursday of November.

Strict rules govern what can be sold as Beaujolais nouveau. Only wine from the regions of Beaujolais and Beaujolais-Villages may use the term, and then only if the wine is pressed from Gamay grapes and matured by a process that produces fermentation in a mere twenty-one days.

For a little wine, Beaujolais nouveau became big business. At one time, restaurateurs all over the world competed to be the first to offer the new vintage. Runners, rickshaws, trucks, helicopters, hot-air balloons, motorcycles, Concorde jets, even elephants were employed to rush a case from the vineyards north of Lyon in time for customers to open a bottle at one minute past midnight on that third Thursday.

Today, the onetime rarity has become a cliché. Sixty-five million bottles are sold worldwide every year, mostly to people who can't tell Cabernet from Kool-Aid. One critic dismissed the wine in its present state as "nothing more than pleasantly tart barroom swill."

But to write it off is to miss the point. If the Beaujolais nouveau had value, it lay in the idea behind it. Like the Romans who ceremonially spilled wine on the ground as an offering to the gods, we drank it as a libation, a sacrifice to the inevitability of change.

Ahead lay hard months from which it would not be so easy to wring a wine as pleasant as this. But winter had its pleasures too. Long before I came here, I read Paul Bowles's evocation of "the hushed, intense cold that lay over the Seine in the early morning, the lavender-gray daylight that filtered down from the damp sky at noon; even on clear days the useless, impossibly distant, small sun." I was ready. Yaseen Khan and the chestnut seller and La Souris Verte and Beaujolais nouveau had prepared the way. And Fabre d'Églantine too, in his fashion. Send on Frimaire, Nivôse, and Pluviôse, and the days of granite, salt, and iron. We would deal with them together.

21

BLOODY DAYS

Acapulco, Mexico. Christmas 1975. 10 p.m. 15°C. In the dark of the hotel balcony overlooking the bay, three guitarists play as the waiter juggles cups and silverware. Lifting a ladle to chest height, he sets it alight and pours burning cognac in a stream of blue flame. The velvet night retreats for a few moments, then closes in once more.

REVISING THE CALENDAR MIGHT HAVE ENDED WITH THE IMPOSI-tion of the metric system on the counting of day and years, but no revolution does things by halves. Powered by Fabre's ambition, the project built up unstoppable momentum.

More than internal disruption, revolutionary France feared invasion, particularly by Catholic Austria and Italy. The threat posed by the pope and the Vatican was more than ideological. France took seriously the possibility of an Italian army invading to free the imprisoned Catholic clergy. In July 1792, amid rumors of such a force headed for Paris, the mob slaughtered almost two hundred imprisoned priests, monks, nuns, and bishops.

Even more were murdered the following September during further riots, ignited in part by Fabre's rabble-rousing speeches to the Convention. Danton deprecated the killings in public, but rationalized in private that they had their favorable side; if there really was a fifth column within Paris, its members would now be too scared to act.

The Reformation in Germany and England may have substituted a more rational style of belief, but in Italy and France the Roman church remained omnipotent. Backing its power was the threat of hellfire, illustrated in church paintings and emphasized repeatedly from the pulpit. Excommunication and the damnation that followed could bring kings crawling in rags to the pope, begging forgiveness for having challenged his omnipotence.

Rooting out any lingering influence of the church came high on the list of revolutionary priorities. Purging the new calendar of all religious doctrine would demonstrate that the French farmer lived and died not according to some superstitious schedule conceived of by foreigners but in response to the turn of the seasons as experienced in his own fields and vineyards.

Having renamed the days of the week to remove their associations with the Gregorian calendar, Fabre turned to the months. Discarding their names, all of which celebrated pagan festivals, he substituted others that evoked the countryside and nature.

The months were given names ending in one of four syllables. Those of fall terminated in "aire," winter months in "ôse," spring months in "al," and summer in "dor."

The first month of the revised calendar, Vendémiaire, coinciding with the grape harvest, or *vendange*, ran from the former September 22 to October 21. It was followed by Brumaire, the month of mists, named for *brume*, the French word for "fog," then by Frimaire, from *frimas* (frost).

Nivôse was snowy, from the Latin for "snow," *nivosus*. Pluviôse—from the Latin *pluviosus*—was rainy, and Ventôse windy, from the Latin *ventosus*.

In Germinal, from the Latin *germinis* (bud), grain germinated. Floréal, from *floreus*, was the month of flowers, followed by Prairial, from *prairie*, the French word for "meadow," which the first explorers gave to the grasslands of the American West.

Finally, the months of high summer concluded with "dor," from *doron*, the Greek word for "gift." Grain was reaped in Messidor, from the Latin *messis* (harvest), while Thermidor, the former August, took its name from the Greek *thermon* (heat), and Fructidor from the Latin *fructus* (fruit), leading back to Vendémiaire.

In the redistribution of days, weeks, and years, a day was left over at the end of each year. These became public holidays for the ordinary citizens, the *sans-culottes*. The consummate adman, Fabre labeled them *sans-culottides*, holidays for the trouserless ones.

La Fête de la Vertu would celebrate good works. La Fête du Génie would recognize talent or skill, and La Fête du Travail honor labor. On La Fête des Récompenses, awards would be made and honors conferred, and a fifth day, La Fête de la Révolution, would honor the achievements of the revolution with solemn splendor and high ritual. On the last holiday, La Fête de l'Opinion, citizens would be permitted to say what they liked about any public figure without risk of prosecution for libel. (Unfortunately the calendar didn't survive long enough for any of these festivals to be celebrated, least of all the last, which promised to be memorable.)

At this point, Fabre and his helpers set down their pens, leaned back, and savored the sense of a task skillfully, even brilliantly completed. On every level, their creation appeared a total success. In offering to the people of France a means of relating their lives to the natural world, the calendar achieved a harmony of intellect and labor that the American poet Walt Whitman, writing nearly a century later of the American ideal, would call "something in the doings of man that corresponds with the broadcast doings of the day and night."

In its embrace of the modern over the antique and its sense of a rational new society, the calendar embodied the purest spirit of the revolution. A kind of poem, it reflected this divine beauty and echoed the music of the spheres. It mirrored the universe as it would one day be metered by Foucault's pendulum: inexorable, essential, eternal.

How could it fail? But as the old—and, in terms of the Republican calendar, politically unacceptable—joke goes, "If you want to see God laugh, show him your plans."

❋ ·22· ❋

APRIL IN PARIS

Malibu, California. August 1988. 2 a.m. 14°C. A chattering crowd fringes the beach as waves of the silver fish called grunion slither ashore, carpeting the zone where water meets sand. As females lay their eggs in the tidal flow, males ejaculate spasmodically into the soup of saltwater, sand, and milt before the ebb carries them, spent, back out to sea. Gleefully, watchers scoop them up in buckets, ingredients for a late supper.

People often ask, "What's the best time to come to Paris?"

Before I moved here, I would have said, "Well, I suppose April," not from conviction but simply because the song "April in Paris" is so ubiquitous that it could be the city's theme. From Ella Fitzgerald and Frank Sinatra to the entire Count Basie band—discovered, in Mel Brooks's comedy western *Blazing Saddles*, blasting it out in the midst of the Arizona desert—it has more than earned its status as a standard. Composer Alec Wilder insists, "This is a perfect theater song. If that sounds too reverent, then I'll reduce the praise to 'perfectly wonderful,' or else say that if it's not perfect, show me why it isn't."

A jazz listener since adolescence, I'd grown up with "April in Paris," but like most things encountered early in life, since taken it for granted.

It comes from an obscure 1932 Broadway show, *Walk a Little Faster.* The composer was Vladimir Dukelsky, who chose to work as Vernon Duke.

The lyrics were by E. Y. "Yip" Harburg, who wrote "Over the Rainbow" but also "Lydia the Tattooed Lady," with its catalog of body art made memorable by Groucho Marx: "Here's Captain Spaulding exploring the Amazon / Here's Godiva but with her pajamas on," not to mention "Here's Nijinsky, doing the rumba. / Here's her social security numba."

"April in Paris" didn't aspire to that degree of invention. Its first few lines—"April in Paris, chestnuts in blossom / Holiday tables under the trees"—produced no frisson of recognition. They didn't even rival another Duke/Harburg collaboration, "Autumn in New York," with its sly couplet "Lovers that bless the dark / On benches in Central Park."

To my surprise, "April in Paris" has an introductory verse, but it's seldom performed. Reading the lyrics, claiming that April brought a "tang of wine in the air," I wasn't surprised.

Wondering if I was missing some nuance, I ran the lyrics past my gastronome friend Boris. Able to spot the bogus at a hundred meters, he didn't disappoint.

"'The tang of wine'? Who wrote this? Had he ever even *been* to Paris?"

AVRIL

... Robe noire et cheveux blancs,
Tête calme, douce et franche,
Grand'Maman, dont le front penche,
Promène ses pas tremblants.

... Avec ses yeux endiablants,
Cheveux noirs et robe blanche,
Germaine au bout d'une branche
A vu des bourgeons troublants.

... Et la petite Lolotte,
L'hiver dernier si pâlotte,
Joue et court, hors de péril...

... Si l'on en croit ces trois âges,
Décorons le sieur Avril,
Grand peintre de paysages.

MICHAEL.

A melancholy vision of April in Paris.

"In fact, Duke lived here for years," I said. "He wrote a ballet for Diaghilev, was a friend of Prokofiev. But Harburg . . . I doubt it."

I didn't mention Lydia and her tattoos. Why call down more scorn on my head?

"And 'chestnuts in blossom, holiday tables under the trees'? Those are hardly unique to April."

He was right. The *marron* (chestnut), Paris's most common tree, flowered throughout the spring. And as for "holiday tables under the trees," April has no monopoly on those. A blizzard needs to be blowing before café owners take in the highly profitable tables and chairs ranged along the sidewalk. Some hand out blankets for clients to wrap around their legs and keep right on serving even when the unprotected parts of their patrons begin to turn blue.

By 1952, the fantasy of April in Paris was comprehensively blown. The writers of *April in Paris*, a film released that year starring Doris Day, seemed actually to know the city, since they poked fun at the whole idea. Day, a new arrival in France and eager to experience its widely advertised warmth, gaiety, and romance, convinces her leading man to sit outside at a café, even when a waiter, teeth chattering, urges them to move inside. When Day refuses, he takes cover himself, telling them he'll be back in July.

A journalist friend had other reasons for disliking "April in Paris."

"I can't tell you how *tired* I am of that song," he said. "Every year, they dust it off on the first day of April. On TV they play it over a montage of cafés and flowers, all from last summer, of course.

It's a *marron*, a chestnut." He had a sudden thought. "You know, don't you, that's why anything boring—an old joke, or this TV thing—is called a 'chestnut'? There used to be an old *marron* tree in the Tuileries that was the first to flower every spring. In England you have the first call of the cuckoo bird, and in America that rat thing—"

"A groundhog, actually," I said. "Name's Punxsutawney Phil."

"*C'est vrai? Merde alors!*" He raised his eyebrows, partly at the name but mostly at the fact that I should know about it.

"Well, in Paris," he went on, "the first sign of spring was this *marron* flowering. So some reporter was sent to write a piece about it. Usually it was the *stagiaire*." Obviously he had once been such a trainee himself. "A horrible job. What can one say that hasn't been said a thousand times before? *C'est ennuyeux*. So that's why we say that anything like that is a *marron*, a chestnut."

Worse and worse. The credibility of April in Paris as the inspiration for a song was evaporating before my eyes. So why would Duke write something that so poorly described a city he must have known intimately? Could it be no more than the fact that "April in Paris" fell more agreeably on the ear than "March," "May," "June," or "July in Paris"?

As I discovered after more research, it may all have been the fault of writer Dorothy Parker, a friend of lyricist Harburg. A cynic's cynic and a mistress of acid wordplay—"If all the women [at this party] were laid end to end, I wouldn't be at all surprised"—Parker was a poet of the glass-half-empty persuasion. Life to her was one long disappointment, its pain assuaged by liberal applications of gin and sex.

According to one account, Parker was within earshot when Vernon Duke referred to Robert Browning's poem "Home-Thoughts, from Abroad" as a possible theme for a song. Was there a tune to be had from this dithyramb to the English spring, with its famous first lines "Oh, to be in England / Now that April's there"?

Through her tenth martini, darkly, Parker saw nothing appealing about England in April. The fogs, the rain, and, my dear, the *people!*

But France . . . Now that was something else.

"Oh, to be in *Paris*," she murmured, "now that April's there."

And from this bitter soil a song germinated? Isn't it pretty to think so.

A BOY NAMED WHEELBARROW

Matsue, western Japan. September 1982. 2 p.m.
10°C. Carp, dead white skin patched with orange and
black, peer up, mouths pouting, from their shallow
pond. Beyond, the ancient castle's moat, now carpeted
with green lawn, is filled with white tents, in and out
of which slip exquisite women in kimonos of white silk
also patterned with black and orange.

For all its faults, the Gregorian calendar had done good work.

Partly an almanac, a guide to the seasons, it reminded the rural population of their duties to both nature and the church. Even peasants who couldn't write their names could count on their fingers and so knew it was a sin to eat meat on the fifth day of the week and that you must attend mass on the seventh day, eat less for a precise period preceding Easter, and post the banns in the church for a certain number of weeks before you married.

Others had already worked on developing another almanac for the illiterate. In 1588, Jehan Tabourot, a scholar who wrote as

Thoinot Arbeau, published *The Compot or Manual Calendar, by Which All Persons Can Easily Learn and Forecast the Passage of the Sun, and the Moon, and Similarly the Fixed and Moveable Feasts Which We Have to Celebrate in the Church, Following the Correction Ordered by Our Holy Pope Gregoire XIII.*

It showed how since, conveniently, we have the same number of joints in our fingers as there are months, the simplest peasant could use his hands to keep track of the ecclesiastical year.

Late in the eighteenth century, someone suggested that a pack of playing cards could serve the same purpose. The idea survived into the twentieth century, to be taken up in the 1940s in an improbable quarter.

In 1948, an obscure country singer named T. Texas Tyler recorded a recitation called "The Deck of Cards." To the quasi-devotional noodling of an electric organ, Tyler described a soldier who took out a deck of cards at a religious service.

Disciplined by an officer, the soldier explained that he used the cards as a prayer book and almanac. The ace reminded him of the one true God, the two of the Old and New Testaments, the three of the trinity, and so on. As for the almanac function, the fifty-two cards equaled the number of weeks in a year, the twelve cards of a suit the number of months, and the four suits the number of weeks in a month.

Critics were quick to spot inconsistencies. If an ace signifies the one true God, how does one account for the existence of three others? Such questions, not to mention the holier-than-thou tone— Tyler ends by declaring, "I was that soldier"—didn't inhibit sales of the record, which rose to No. 2 on the hit parade and was widely imitated. The church didn't object. Like Tabourot's finger calendar, "The Deck of Cards" implied that the divine was present even in the simplest elements of nature, a belief the church was keen to encourage.

Fabre also understood the importance of the calendar as an almanac, and promised to incorporate this function in the new version. "As the calendar is something that we use so often," he somewhat patronizingly assured the Convention, "we must take advantage of this frequency of use to put elementary notions of agriculture before the people—to show the richness of nature, to make them love the fields, and to methodically show them the order of the influences of the heavens and of the products of the earth."

One important function of the Gregorian calendar was in the naming of children. By law, parents could choose only from names that appeared in the official calendar. This meant that children were automatically recruited by the church from the moment they were baptized. A few parents in the Caribbean, from either ignorance or defiance, christened their sons "Toussaint," which signified the feast of *tous saints* (All Saints' Day). Others injected individuality by doubling up, calling their children Jean-Luc or Marie-Claire, or exploited a technicality by choosing Jean-Baptiste, i.e., John the Baptist. But most toed the ecclesiastical line.

Fabre's solution was characteristically extreme: "We thought that the nation, after having kicked out this canonized mob from its calendar, must replace it with the objects that make up the true riches of the nation, worthy objects not from a cult but from agriculture-useful products of the soil, the tools that we use to cultivate it, and the domestic animals, our faithful servants in these works."

Accordingly, every day in the Republican calendar was renamed for a flower or plant, each *décade* (week) for a tool or object one might see around the farm, and each *demi-décade* (the former fortnight) for a domestic animal: "more precious, without doubt," suggested Fabre, "to the eye of reason than the beatified skeletons pulled from the catacombs of Rome."

This proposal confronted the calendar's framers with their biggest challenge. Despite his pose as Old Farmer Philippe, Fabre probably couldn't identify more than a few common plants or flowers and wouldn't have known a shovel from a spade. He hurriedly recruited an expert.

André Thouin (pronounced *Twain*) supervised the Jardin du Roi, the Royal Garden, the finest botanical museum in the world. Sprawling across the left bank of the Seine, its walls enclosed hothouses, orangeries, groves of trees, and plantations of fruits and flowers brought back from the far corners of the world.

Thouin learned botany from his father, head gardener before him, and from Georges-Louis Leclerc, Comte de Buffon, who pioneered the systematic identification and cataloging of animals and

Botanist André Thouin.

plants. Recognizing his talent, Buffon recommended him to take over after the death of Thouin Senior in 1764.

Thouin made the Royal Garden famous across Europe. He introduced numerous new plant varieties to France, sometimes at personal risk. The spices and exotic plants imported by the first European travelers in India and beyond had alerted Europe's governments to the commercial value of botany. In 1794 and 1806, when France invaded the low countries, Thouin led raiding parties in the wake of the army, "rescuing" (i.e., looting) the specimens collected by Dutch botanists in Asia and the Pacific.

Thouin corresponded with gardeners everywhere, and with such thinkers as Jean-Jacques Rousseau, whose philosophy of simplicity and harmony with nature he followed. He also became friendly with future US president Thomas Jefferson, who praised his research as "well worthy of one whose time and great talents for that science have been so much devoted to its improvement." They regularly exchanged parcels of seeds for trees, grasses, and exotic fruits and vegetables. Among these were tomatoes, familiar for centuries as a decorative plant but believed to be poisonous until soldiers from Mediterranean Marseilles brought the fruit to Paris in 1789.

Almost excessively modest, Thouin refused to wear anything but the simple smock recommended by Rousseau. Even when awarded the Légion d'Honneur, he declined to display its red ribbon in his buttonhole, saying it was "not appropriate to my gardener's shirt." Appointed a professor, he agreed, reluctantly, to give morning lectures, expecting only a handful amateurs. Instead, he found himself addressing the assembled gardeners of stately homes and horticulturists from all over Europe.

It's likely that Thouin had reservations about the Republican calendar and the man behind it from the start. But Voltaire's injunction in *Candide* to "cultivate our own gardens" before giving advice to others had served him well, and he was not about to change. He supplied the hundreds of plant and animal names demanded by Fabre, and left it to him how they were used.

If Fabre used a system to match plants and flowers to specific days, nobody has ever unraveled it. The *demi-décades* of Floréal, for example, the former mid-April to mid-May, were puzzlingly represented among domestic animals by the nightingale and the silkworm The agricultural implements of its three *décades* were the rake, the garden hoe, and the shepherd's crook, on none of which, it's reasonable to assume, Fabre had ever laid a hand.

Individual days were named *chêne* (oak), *fougère* (fern), *aubépine* (hawthorn), *ancolie* (columbine), and *muguet* (lily of the valley). When the compilers ran short, Thouin rummaged up another obscure plant or object, though he was often on shaky ground, as with *armoise* (mugwort) and *topinambour* (Jerusalem artichoke).

Although every day in the warm months of the year had its own signifying flower or plant, the coldest month, Nivôse, stumped Thouin, since barely anything green stuck its head above ground then. Instead, in a final complication, Fabre assigned each of its days not a plant or flower but a mineral or animal product. These included *granit* (granite), *lave* (lava), and *fumier* (dung).

The concept of naming children for plants, flowers and domestic objects, attractive in principle, proved impossible in practice. Among other difficulties, such names were seen as suiting women far more than men. Girls could choose from a cornucopia of fruits and flowers—Violette, Poire, Garance, Amaryllis—but unless you wanted to call your son Wheelbarrow, saints' names remained the preferred choice for boys.

In 1803 Napoléon, as part of his new agreement with the church, restored the law requiring parents to choose from the names of the saints alone. By and large, it still applies. Regional names are more common today, particularly Celtic adoptions such as Gaëlle and Yannick, but fruit and flower names turn up rarely. An attempt to christen a girl Fraise (strawberry) was overturned in the courts by a compassionate judge who pointed out that *"ramener ta fraise"* (literally "pull in your strawberry"—the equivalent of "mind your own business,") would doom a girl called Fraise to a miserable childhood. The parents compromised on Fraisier—"strawberry shortcake."

Within a few weeks of the calendar becoming official, people in all walks of life were complaining. In practice, the revised system was absurdly cumbersome. June 19, 1794, old style, became Messidor 1 of Year III, or, for those who could neither read nor count, Day *Seigle* (rye) of Week Mule in fortnight Shawm (a woodwind musical instrument).

Had Fabre been aware of the calendar's unpopularity among

ordinary people, he might have delayed its general introduction, particularly since the project had already served his purpose of making him famous. At the time, however, he had other things on his mind. His life—lived increasingly, like those of all public men, in the shadow of the guillotine—was slipping out of control.

❊ ·24· ❊

HOT HOT HOT

*Fouras, Charente, Atlantic coast of southwestern France.
February 2010. 8°C. Dazed from a night of wind, locals
straggle down to the concrete esplanade and stare, disbe-
lieving, at the void once occupied by their beach, carried
away by the storm surge of Hurricane Xynthia. Concrete
stairways that once touched the sand now hang in emptiness two meters above black river mud.*

ONE THING ON WHICH I ASSUMED EVERYONE COULD AGREE: IF
there was a worst month to visit Paris, it was surely August.

That was the month when anyone with the most feeble pretext
locked the office and left town. In resorts all over France, seaside
hotels, apartment buildings, and even campsites came to life, filled
with people fleeing the cities.

Lying like a musty quilt across its roofs, the heat of August sti-
fled every quality in which Paris in particular took pride. Cafés and
restaurants closed, museums went on half-time, and in the few shops
that remained open, languid vendeuses made no secret of longing to
join their friends in Le Touquet or Antibes. The essentials of daily

life disappeared. "On the last day of July," confided a friend, "everyone forced to remain in Paris buys ten fresh baguettes and puts them in the freezer. It's the last edible bread they'll see for a month."

Until refrigeration made cold drinks commonplace, street sellers flourished, in particular those offering Coco, a concoction of lemon juice and water flavored with licorice. At *guinguettes*, open-air bars, thirsty men guzzled liters of beer, then collapsed under the nearest tree to sleep through the stifling afternoon.

Heat induced the apathy known as cafard. One could medicate it—with sex, for instance—but the result was often self-defeating. As temperatures climbed, relationships were stretched to the breaking point.

Paris emptied by degrees. People with children slipped away in July, when school holidays began. Others delayed, but never beyond mid-August. "Tomorrow is the Feast of the Assumption," wrote Canadian writer and longtime Parisian expat Mavis Gallant, "and the whole of Catholic Europe will shut down its cities and make for mountains and beaches. Any tourist caught in Madrid, Vienna, Rome, or Paris on the 15th of August can vouch for what 'empty city' means."

In her attitude to Paris in August, as in much else, Gallant was the exception. She relished the emptiness, and—particularly after arthritis left her bent, shuffling, and mostly housebound—she often chose to remain right through August in her little apartment on rue Jean Ferrandi. She wrote about it in 1993 for the online magazine *Slate*:

Coco soft-drink seller in the Paris streets, 1900s.

Keep the beer coming, 1890s caricature.

"It bothers people—friends, I mean—that I spend every August in Paris. They think it is unhealthy, surely lonely, probably eccentric. The truth is that I prefer being in a city, all the time, more and more, and 'city' means Paris. I am frequently offered an airy room in a country house, in Normandy, in Brittany, and sometimes the house itself. I am assured that I would be able to work in peace, that no one would ever bother me, that I could just turn up for meals. Thank you, no. . . ."

To equate anonymity with freedom is a particularly Parisian trait. At the *bals musettes* of the late nineteenth and early twentieth centuries, dancers behaved like neighbors who nod to one another in the street but never introduce themselves. Even at the small neighborhood *bals*, which could simply be at cafés with the owner playing an accordion for dancing, one never revealed one's name. Clinging to total strangers, body grinding against body in the jigging dance known as the *java*, they still remained silent. In 1922 Ernest and Hadley Hemingway danced at such a neighborhood *bal*, the rule of silence a convenience for new arrivals like them who spoke no French.

Not that Paris in August is without its pleasures, but those that exist are, like those of the *bal musette*, perfumed with decadence. Many Parisians don't bother with curtains, preferring to control heat and light with shutters. When, at morning or evening, these are folded back to admit cooler air, both voyeurs and exhibitionists are spoiled for choice, a taste that helps explain the popularity among the French of Alfred Hitchcock's films *Rear Window* and *Vertigo*, celebrations of the watchers and the watched.

Mavis Gallant used this time to exercise a slightly perverse pleasure in observing the oddities of her neighbors. One incident would not have been out of place in one of her acerbic short stories. Kept awake all night by a barking poodle in another apartment, she reported it to the police, who found that the seventeen-year-old son of the family, alone in Paris while the family was on holiday, would leave the dog unattended all night while he went out to party. "Yesterday I met them both, boy and dog, in the street," Gallant wrote. "Nothing was said, but he stopped, pointed to the poodle, raised the leash, as if it were evidence in a trial, and gave me a look that conveyed apology, bewilderment, and gloom."

25

RE-ENTER FABRE

Cambridge, England. April 1971. 3 p.m. 14°C. The punt glides downstream, a friend standing on the stern and casually manipulating the two-meter pole. The college buildings of honey stone that we pass seem to embody intellectual superiority. Nothing here but ideas has any real importance. The river implies otherwise, its languid flow evoking Rupert Brooke's "stream mysterious . . . / Green as a dream and deep as Death."

ONCE FABRE D'ÉGLANTINE BECAME KNOWN AS A POLITICIAN AND speculator, he discarded the image of a poet, rebranding himself as a man-about-town. His open shirt and casual jacket gave way to a silk cravat, surcoat, and vest. A coiffeur fluffed his hair into a bouffant. He also took to carrying a lorgnette, a pair of eyeglasses on a handle, through which he would peer at the proceedings of the Convention and the Club des Cordeliers as if they were stage comedies performed for his amusement, a habit that irritated his fellow members.

He had his portrait painted by the aging but fashionable Jean-Baptiste Greuze, and promptly parodied the painter in one of his verse comedies. His last work, *The Proud Fool*, presented in August 1792, went even further—mocking the revolution, or at least its more pompous poseurs. Few were amused.

Fabre had already begun accumulating a personal fortune by speculating in shares of the Compagnie Française des Indes Orientales. Inspired by the British and Dutch East India Companies, which gave those nations access to the wealth of India and East Asia, Louis XIV started this French equivalent to build trading posts on the subcontinent and import its spices and fabrics. The revolution's leaders planned to stamp out such survivals from the bad old days of the monarchy, but until they got around to it the company continued to generate a healthy income for its stockholders.

Danton helped Fabre gain a place on the commission charged with supplying the army, a notorious pork barrel that Fabre exploited recklessly. By buying inferior goods but billing the government at top price, he pocketed 40,000 livres, a small fortune. A disgusted Robespierre claimed that the boots supplied to the troops were of such poor quality that they barely lasted half a day before falling to pieces.

For the moment, Fabre's association with Danton protected him, but his mentor was also under attack, suspected of skimming from the fortunes of those aristocrats sent to the guillotine. Each time Danton rose in the Convention to speak, opponents shouted, "The accounts, the accounts!"

Busy with business deals, Fabre didn't have time to publicize his involvement in the calendar project. Instead, he had others do it for him. At his instigation, Michel de Cubières, a prolific self-styled *poète de la révolution*, composed an eleven-page ode celebrating the new calendar and hinting broadly that all involved, but in particular Fabre, deserved some honor and even a little profit:

> *The illustrious citizen deserves his reward.*
> *Kings offer gold, popes forgiveness,*
> *But the ordinary citizen, recognizing victory,*
> *Places laurel on the warrior's brow.*
> *This true brightness puts crowns to shade.*

On September 23, 1793, Charles-Gilbert Romme, technically head of the calendar commission, formally presented it to the Convention. After some perfunctory debate, it was adopted on October 24.

Barely anyone took any notice. That year had become the first annus horribilis of the new France. In May and June, the Jacobins, supporters of Robespierre and opponents of Danton, won a majority in the Convention. On July 13, Jean-Paul Marat, a leader of the Montagnards and one of Danton's most effective colleagues, was murdered, stabbed in his bath by Charlotte Corday, a supporter of the moderate Girondin party.

Marat's tirades in his newspaper, *L'Ami du peuple*, had fanned a growing sense of desperation throughout France as foreign armies threatened its borders. With almost unlimited powers to convict and execute without trial, the Committee of Public Safety crushed even the slightest expressions of dissent.

Fabre had been one of those who supported Marat in denouncing a "foreign plot" against the Republic. The denunciation set off a barrage of accusations that heightened the prevailing paranoia and accelerated the frequency of public executions, now a daily occurrence across the country.

Fabre continued to speculate in East India Company shares. When in 1793 the Committee of Public Safety finally got around to banning all joint-stock companies, he smelled an even greater profit in winding up its affairs. Officials, their palms well greased, allowed its directors, rather than the government, to liquidate the company. In this fire sale of assets, the insiders cleaned up.

This was a swindle too far. When Robespierre made the details public, a heckler at the Club des Cordeliers pointed at Fabre and shouted, "To the guillotine with him!" Paling, Fabre dropped his lorgnette. For the first time he realized that his influential friends didn't make him immune. He hurriedly resigned his seat in the Convention, but it was too late. Robespierre launched a campaign to discredit him and the other so-called indulgents who urged an end to revolutionary extremism. The stage was set for the last act not only of the life of Fabre d'Églantine but also of the revolution itself.

26

SINGIN' IN THE RAIN

Studio Babelsberg, Potsdam, Germany. February 2006. 2 p.m. 2 degrees below zero C. On the back lot, set designers have meticulously re-created a city street in middle Europe, c. 1920. A beat after the director waves "Action," wet flakes of snow begin to fall. This is, after all, the studio that made Metropolis, The Blue Angel, *and* M. *As Conrad Veidt's Nazi colonel purrs in* Casablanca, *"I expected no less."*

I T'S ONE OF THOSE MILESTONE MOMENTS IN CINEMA HISTORY. GENE Kelly, delirious with newfound love for Debbie Reynolds, stomps and splashes around Los Angeles in the pouring rain, even pausing under a drainpipe to let water gush over his head. Maurice Chevalier had done much the same with Ann Sothern in the "Rhythm of the Rain" number for a 1935 film called *Folies Bergère de Paris,* but Kelly's version put that to shame.

Few of us have such happy memories of being caught in a downpour. An instinct as ancient as the cave dweller drives us to seek shelter, however insubstantial, leaving the world of water to the fish, snails, and frogs. A traditional yardstick of intelligence decrees of the stupid, "Didn't have the sense to come in out of the rain."

This was what I mused, anyway, as I retreated deeper into a doorway in Montparnasse, the better to take advantage of its minimal shelter. It was February 14—Pluviôse 26 in the Republican calendar, in a month well named for its rain. Finding that the plant of the day was *guède* contributed to an overall sense of dankness. When Britain was largely bogs and rocks, my Celtic ancestors daubed their bodies with the blue dye it produced. They called it "woad."

From across the street a youngish man sprinted toward me, sheltering something bulky under a voluminous coat. A tenant of this building? If so, he could probably buzz both of us into the vestibule, where I could wait out the storm in comfort. But his imploring look signaled that he was just another pedestrian, so I shuffled aside to make room.

To shake the rain from his coat, he had to let go of what he'd been protecting. With a hollow *bong*, a battered acoustic guitar dropped a few centimeters to the stone step. Almost certainly he was a street musician, a busker.

"Singin' in the rain?" I said.

He looked blank. "*Comment?*"

I scrabbled for the translation. "Er, *chantons sous la pluie?*"

Clearly baffled, he peered at the rainy sky, then at me, and screwed up his brow to mime bafflement. Had I struck the one young *Parisien* who wasn't into movies?

"C'est pas important," I said.

We stood in silence for a few moments, until a lull in the shower cued him to pick up the guitar again and, with a nod, sprint off downhill toward the Jardins du Luxembourg.

I was in no hurry. And rain was still sufficiently exotic for me, after years of Australian and Californian summers, to be enjoyable in itself. It wasn't until I went to live in Los Angeles that "Singin' in the Rain" made sense. To dance under a Californian downpour was simply to celebrate its novelty.

Once the guitarist left, I realized my guess about him being a busker was probably wrong. He was French, while almost all buskers, in common with people writing in cafés or shopping at Louis Vuitton, are foreign.

Blame this on the complex relationship between Parisians and the street. Where in other cities the distinction between At Home and In Public is clearly defined, in Paris the nature of public and private space is a matter of constant redefinition.

Most of us look on the streets as dead ground, to be passed through as quickly as possible on our way to our true destination. In Los Angeles, I had barely put foot to pavement. To the French, however, the street is a destination in itself. Parisians dress to go out, even if just to the supermarket. Entering a shop, a café, even a bus, they greet the proprietor or driver as if visiting a friend in his home. Conversations of startling intimacy take place in the hearing of other pedestrians or passengers, and there is no city in the world

Buskers in Paris, 1870s.

where a more intimate relationship can be initiated by eyes meeting eyes in that glance of mutual interest.

Few Frenchmen would insinuate a guitar or accordion into this intricate cultural exchange. Instead, metro passengers are serenaded by octets of Peruvians warbling on panpipes and pickup bands of

Neil Hornick and the Sidewalkers in Copenhagen.

American students doing upbeat versions of "Softly, as in a Morning Sunrise."

If Parisians sing in the street, it's generally a form of advertising. Édith Piaf became a pavement vocalist to attract spectators for her father, a street acrobat and contortionist. In the 1920s, song pluggers cruised working-class suburbs. Selecting a courtyard with good acoustics, they sang a few choruses of the latest ballad to coax people to their windows, then sold them a copy of the sheet music. Albert Préjean played such a person in René Clair's film *Sous les toits de Paris* (*Under the Roofs of Paris*). Many Paris buskers today follow the tradition, selling CDs of their work.

The voices of street performers seldom lasted long. Singing in all weathers and at maximum volume strained the untrained voice, battering it into a grating growl well suited to the songs of poverty and despair written and performed by Aristide Bruant and Jehan Rictus, both of whom wrote of the streets but found their audience in the cabarets of Montmartre. Édith Piaf too was fortunate. A passing club owner recognized her talent, rescued her, disciplined her voice, coaxed her into her trademark little black dress, and made her famous.

These days, busking in Paris is strictly controlled. The city issues only three hundred permits each year, and these only after applicants have passed an audition in front of three fellow performers, the least sympathetic of judges.

It's no game for the faint of heart. Britain's Henry VIII swore to "whip unlicensed minstrels and players, fortune-tellers, pardoners and fencers, as well as beggars." In Hugo's novel *Notre Dame de Paris*, the street performer Esmerelda is about to be hanged as a witch when she's rescued by the bell ringer Quasimodo. More recently, when Édith Piaf's mentor refused to sell her contract to some old friends from her street-singing days, they murdered him, possibly with her connivance.

Once on the street, modern buskers face a variety of risks, including being hassled and robbed by rivals and mocked and abused by drunken football fans, not to mention having the *gendarmerie* arrest them for performing outside their assigned location.

Despite this, the tradition has survived and flourished, even creating its own mythology. London buskers traditionally work the movie queues on Leicester Square or those for theaters on nearby Saint Martin's Lane. A 1938 film, *Sidewalks of London* (also known as *Saint Martin's Lane*), suggested that some might be stars waiting to be discovered—easy to believe when one of them is a young Vivien Leigh.

But most buskers are less interested in a theatrical career than in exploiting a modest talent for cash. My friend Neil busked across Europe in the 1960s, including a few turns on the *trottoirs* of Paris. I asked him what he recalled of the experience. Inevitably, his memories involved the weather.

"Paris in sunshine has a luster of its own. I lived close to the Luxembourg Gardens and loved strolling there, as well as dawdling and browsing at the book and postcard stalls along the Seine. Clearly there was no point in busking when the weather was bad—always disappointing, that—though punters queuing under an awning on *la rive gauche* in the drizzle in order to see the latest *nouvelle vague* movie appreciated a bit of live entertainment, even if on the raucous side.

"Otherwise, my only other weather-tinged memory concerns the beautiful German girl who took a fancy to me singing by the Seine and soon became my live-in girlfriend (in her *chambre de bonne*). One sunny, if windy, day we joined a group of friends on a picnic excursion. At one point during this *déjeuner sur l'herbe*, we covered ourselves from waist to toe with a light blanket, beneath which Ulrike contrived, to my surprise, to bring me to climax with her bare feet while our friends continued unknowingly to eat, drink, and chatter."

Forget chestnuts and *al fresco* cafes. Such sensuous idylls as this celebrate what is truly distinctive about Paris in the spring.

27

PINUPS

Near Épernay, region of the Marne. June 18, 1944.
The supreme allied commander notices that the sector
of the advance controlled by the French is lagging
behind the others. An intelligence officer is sent to dis-
cover the reason. He finds the entire French high com-
mand in a tent, bent over a copy of the Atlas des vins
de France. *They are planning a route that will take*
them past every great vineyard in Champagne.

How could anyone have seriously believed that French
farmers would understand the Republican calendar, let alone embrace it? All had been brought up within the sound of church bells.
Married in the church, they named and raised their children in the
church and were buried by the church. Its influence was not to be
expunged with the stroke of a pen.

Had the calendar commission included a farmer, merchant, or
tradesman, they would have seen immediately that their creation
rested on an illusion. Farmers knew from experience the importance

of seasons and the weather. The biblical injunction to respect "a time to sow and a time to reap" left dates and times to be interpreted according to a sense of the seasons that needed no calendar except the one the farmer wrote for himself.

Given time, wiser heads within the Convention would have allowed the scheme to languish. But the circumstances that created it also blinded the creators to its faults. For a nation that could in a few years go from a monarchy to a republic by the most direct route, that of exterminating its ruling class, anything was possible. Some of the revolution's innovations enjoyed surprising success. The metric system would soon be in use across Europe. And the guillotine, only introduced in 1792, became almost overnight an unignorable feature of French political life.

Over the next few years, some parts of the new calendar were enacted, others ignored. At the same time, people were put to work publicizing its merits. One man would do more than anyone to bring Fabre's creation to life, however briefly.

Louis Lafitte was twenty years younger than Fabre. The two never met. Yet Lafitte would put faces to what were just names in the original calendar, and in doing so, humanize it for an international audience.

In 1791, as a young artist at the end of a punishing four-year course at the École des Beaux-Arts, Lafitte won the prestigious Prix de Rome, entitling him to a year of study, all expenses paid, in the Italian capital. In Rome, he worked at the Villa Medici until deteriorating relations between France and Italy made life uncomfortable for Frenchmen there. In 1793 he moved to Florence, where he waited out the Terror as a teacher before returning to France.

Lafitte won his Prix de Rome with a classic history painting of an incident from the Punic Wars, a canvas crowded with heroic figures, meticulously painted drapery, and painstakingly depicted architecture, a style hopelessly unfashionable in a new and aggressively working-class France. With a wife and daughter to support, Lafitte took work where he could find it, painting murals, decorating private homes, and illustrating books. (There was a special frisson for me to discover that he had lived and worked on rue de l'Odéon, just a few doors away from our home.)

His fortunes changed in 1796, when a publisher issuing a new edition of the Republican calendar commissioned twelve paintings to illustrate the months.

Until the revolution, only religious illustrations had been permitted in almanacs and calendars. Even after 1789, editions of the calendar favored the politically respectable. For a 1794 printing, Philibert-Louis Debucourt provided an austere neoclassical illustration showing Marianne, the spirit of the revolution, paging through the Book of Nature as a cherub takes notes. In the frontispiece for another edition, Marianne descends the steps of a temple at the foot of which lie the corpses of other calendar makers, clutching their discredited creations.

Perhaps seeing an opportunity to re-establish himself on the Paris art scene, Lafitte took a radically different line. From a memory filled with voluptuous images from Italy, he created something entirely

The new Republic rewrites the calendar.

new: a panorama of the French countryside and its female inhabitants as no person in the street, let alone any farmer, had ever seen them.

Each of his paintings featured an attractive young woman, lightly dressed, posed with an animal, plant, flower, or implement chosen from those listed by Fabre. A brief poem under each illustration underlined its significance, generally with a double entendre.

Lafitte's images were bold. Doves cuddle up to the dark-haired beauty of Germinal, spreading their wings across her breasts. The pensive brunette representing Prairial fingers two more of these birds nestling on her pubic area.

Thermidor, the month of heat, is accorded the most frank image of all. In an unsubtle evocation of the legend of Leda, ravished by Zeus disguised as a swan, it shows such a bird, one webbed foot planted in the woman's crotch, extending its sinuously phallic neck at full length over the young woman's naked breasts. To one side, a watching satyr, part of a bronze cup, appears to be engaged in some uncomfortable act of self-abuse.

After having the images engraved on copper by Salvatore Tresca and the reproductions colored by hand, the publisher, scenting a bestseller, printed a second deluxe version "for art lovers and connoisseurs." Printed on transparent oiled paper, it allowed Lafitte's images to be displayed backlit in the style of a stained-glass window.

In effect, Lafitte had created the first pinup calendar. His work foreshadowed countless peekaboo beauties in skimpy clothing, or none at all, who would decorate locker rooms and workshops for the next two hundred years.

Thermidor. *Leda and the swan, reinterpreted by Louis Lafitte.*

28

DRUNK IN CHARGE

*Pont Alexandre III, Paris. February. 0°C. As an icy
dust of snow swirls along the sidewalks, Japanese couples pose for wedding photographs with a background
of the seventeenth-century Hôtel des Invalides. Grooms
in dove-gray cutaways and brides in off-the-shoulder
gowns of white tulle grin ecstatically even as their teeth
chatter. Above them, unseen, the giant gilded figures
of Law and the State struggle to restrain the rearing
winged horses representing aspects of Fame, but the
newlyweds are too cold to care.*

ONE MORNING IN 2010, WALKING DOWN RUE FÉROU, A FEW MIN-
utes away from our apartment, I found a man balanced precariously
on a ladder three meters in the air. He was painting words on the
high stone wall around the former seminary, now the Centre des
Finances Publiques (the tax office).

Rue Férou, a short, narrow lane running from Place Saint-
Sulpice to the Luxembourg Gardens, has more artistic significance
than most Paris thoroughfares. When the American surrealist Man

Ray returned to Paris from the United States in 1951 with his new wife, Juliet, they shared a tiny apartment there. Next door, Ernest Hemingway lived for a few years with his second wife, Pauline, before they moved to Key West in 1929.

Distracted by these other associations, I looked back at the painter and realized for the first time what he was painting. It was a poem: Arthur Rimbaud's "Le Bateau ivre" ("The Drunken Boat").

In 1871, in a city battered by the Franco-Prussian War and the anarchist uprising of the Commune, seventeen-year-old runaway Arthur Rimbaud—delinquent, petty thief, absinthe drinker, hashish smoker, and sometime lover of fellow poet Paul Verlaine—recited his poem in public for the first time, in a room above the café on the other side of the square.

In the poet's imagining, he isn't a passenger on the boat but the boat itself, drifting in alien seas and beaching on islands of a strangeness unimaginable in Europe.

> *I've struck Floridas, you know, beyond belief,*
> *Where eyes of panthers in human skins*
> *Merge with the flowers! Rainbow bridles, beneath*
> *The seas' horizon, stretched out to shadowy fins!*

Soon after writing it, Rimbaud left for Africa, abandoning poetry for the life of a merchant. His poems, in particular "Le Bateau ivre," are glimpses of that portion of the national soul that the French hesitate to acknowledge, since its irrationality offends their belief in order and logic. No surprise that Rimbaud would be embraced by those intellectual smash-and-grab men, the surrealists.

Climbing down, the painter introduced himself as Jan Willem Bruins. He intended, he said, to paint all one hundred lines of Rimbaud's text on this wall. His painstaking workmanship and the grid of pencil lines on the stone signaled that he was no mere graffiti artist. Though like most taggers he worked in words, not pictures, he didn't spray his paint. (The best-known French tagger calls himself "Jef Aérosol.") Instead, he used materials that were old even when illustrators were laboriously illuminating manuscripts in the building on the other side of the wall.

Bruins differed in another way from Aérosol and the rest of the taggers: he had permission. The Tegen-Beeld Foundation began in Leiden. After it funded the painting of 110 poems in public places around the town, it extended its program outside the Netherlands, starting with Paris and "Le Bateau ivre."

"Well, you chose the right place," I said.

Across the square, we could see the red awning of the Café de la Mairie, where Rimbaud read the poem for the first time and where, later, Djuna Barnes and Henry Miller hung out and Man Ray sometimes ate breakfast.

Over the next few weeks, I often dropped in on Bruins to check on his progress.

The fact that the poem dealt with the sea and the seasons made perfect sense. There could hardly be a better illustration of that national preoccupation, and the degree to which France differed from Anglo-Saxons in its view of the elements.

Was there a poem in English that viewed the sea with anything like the imagination of "Le Bateau ivre"? I could think of only one: G. K. Chesterton's "Lepanto." It celebrated the 1571 battle off Greece in which a coalition led by Don John of Austria defeated the Ottoman Turks. Both sides sailed galleys rowed by slaves—in the case of the Turkish ships, mostly Christians captured during the Crusades.

Drumming this poem into us, the nuns and monks of our school were more concerned with its historical subtext, a classic case of the good guys—i.e., Catholics—defeating the heathens. About that, I could not have cared less. What exhilarated me was its imagery. Errol Flynn in Technicolor didn't even come close.

> *Don John pounding from the slaughter-painted poop,*
> *Purpling all the ocean like a bloody pirate's sloop,*
> *Scarlet running over on the silvers and the golds,*
> *Breaking of the hatches up and bursting of the holds,*
> *Thronging of the thousands up that labour under sea*
> *White for bliss and blind for sun and stunned for liberty.*
> Vivat Hispania!
> Domino Gloria!
> *Don John of Austria*
> *Has set his people free!*

Chesterton wrote this in 1911, exactly forty years after "Le Bateau ivre," but for all the differences in style and form, the poems share a family resemblance. Rarely for the time among British poets, Chesterton was a Catholic, and militant. Whether he and Rimbaud liked it or not, they had fed on the same fruit, drunk at the same well, as had I.

Watching Bruins became my obsession. If I was anywhere near Saint-Sulpice, I detoured to follow his progression. On one of these visits, I noted an oddity.

"You're painting the stanzas from right to left," I said. "Shouldn't you be working from left to right, the way you would read it in a book?"

Bruins put down his brush.

"I thought of that. But, you know . . ." He looked back to Place Saint-Sulpice, then up toward the Luxembourg Gardens. ". . . I felt the poem blew . . ." He made a *swoosh* motion. ". . . *away* from where Rimbaud read it, and along this little street. So that's how I painted it."

After completing his work, he added a PS to explain his thinking. It wasn't necessary. Poetry, like the weather, is its own reason.

A footnote: In all the years since Bruins completed his work, the wall and its poem—in a city where taggers strike largely unchallenged—has never once been defaced by graffiti. It's not only churches that stand on hallowed ground.

29

EXIT FABRE

*Place de la Révolution, Paris. July 17, 1793. 19°C.
Condemned to death for murdering Jean-Paul Marat,
Charlotte Corday goes to the guillotine. A carpenter
working on the scaffold, believing consciousness may
survive in a severed body part, grabs her head by its
hair and slaps the cheeks. Witnesses gasp when the
dead face, some swear, blushes and shows "unequiv-
ocal indignation." Convicted of abusing a corpse, the
carpenter spends three months in prison.*

IT'S AN IRONY OF THE REPUBLICAN CALENDAR THAT BY THE TIME
the average Frenchman became aware of it, Fabre d'Églantine, the
man who helped create it and championed its use, was dead.

From June 1793 through July 1794, 16,594 people were executed
by guillotine in France, 2,639 of them in Paris. On October 16, it
was Marie Antoinette's turn. Though she never denied leaking military secrets to her native country, Austria, the prosecutors added
trumped-up charges that she had organized orgies at Versailles and
even had sex with her young son.

Truth ceased to matter in that climate of suspicion and hatred. Inquisitors asked all suspects the same questions: "What were you worth before the revolution? What are you worth now?" Those who could not prove poverty were automatically condemned.

Robespierre led the witch hunt. "What we need is a single will," he announced. "It must be either Republican or royalist. If it is to be Republican, we must have Republican ministers, Republican papers, Republican deputies, a Republican government." It went without saying that the "single will" must be his.

When too few deputies sided with him, he accused his opponents of treason and had them condemned to death in what became known as the Terror. He explained his policy in terms of the seasons, a comparison the country would instinctively understand. "If virtue be the spring of a popular government in times of peace," he ranted, "the spring of that government during a revolution is virtue combined with terror: virtue, without which terror is destructive; terror, without which virtue is impotent."

The Terror would forever stain the reputation of the revolution, threatening to overshadow its achievements. For the next two centuries, writers outside France—from Charles Dickens in his novel *A Tale of Two Cities* to Baroness Orczy in her stories of the Scarlet Pimpernel—demonized the revolutionaries and glamorized the aristocracy. Danton, the shady aspects of his character conveniently forgotten, emerged in the popular imagination as the people's champion, betrayed and murdered by Robespierre and his young henchman Louis de Saint-Just.

Many who survived the Terror had stories that rivaled fiction. Thomas Paine, British-born author of *Rights of Man*, was imprisoned and condemned. When the guard who chalked the number of the guillotine to which a prisoner would be sent passed by, the door of Paine's cell happened to be open. His number, written by chance on the inside, wasn't visible with the door closed, so he survived.

The survival of the Marquis de Sade was even more miraculous. In 1789, he was already confined to the Bastille at the instigation of his mother-in-law, who persuaded the king to issue a lettre de cachet, a document whereby he could imprison someone indefinitely without trial. Released in 1790, when the Bastille was destroyed and lettres de cachet abolished, Sade sided with the revolution and, now calling himself Citizen Sade, even became a member of the Convention, meanwhile continuing his celebrations of sexual cruelty that inspired the word "sadist." Finally convicted, he spent the rest of his life in mental institutions writing plays, which he staged with other inmates playing the roles. Some dealt with the revolution, most famously the murder of Marat.

The luck that saved Paine and Sade failed for Danton and his supporters. Fabre, as calculating and self-serving as Danton was visionary and patriotic, contributed to his mentor's downfall. As news spread of the East India Company scandal and people called for the directors, including Fabre, to be executed out of hand, Danton went before the Convention to ask that the accused at least be given a fair trial. "Let them be judged before all the people," he asked, "so that the people can know which of them still deserve their trust." To his astonishment, he was shouted down. "You are Fabre's dupe, Danton!" one member yelled. "He has sat by your side. He has cheated the most patriotic of us."

Throughout the winter of 1793–94, Robespierre and Saint-Just picked off Danton's associates. Hoping to retrieve his reputation, Danton supported the purges. In his final speech to the Convention, he drew on the common experience of country people, using wine as a metaphor for revolution. "Frenchmen! Do not take fright at the effervescence of this first stage of liberty," he said. "It is like a strong new wine that ferments until purged of all its froth."

But it was too late. In March 1794, Robespierre sprung his trap. The Committee of Public Safety swore out a warrant for Danton's arrest and those of thirteen others, including Fabre. Danton pinned his hopes on a trial, at which he could employ his oratorical skill to exonerate himself and discredit his accusers. But Robespierre, fearing that Danton's thundering baritone might sway the jury, invoked a new law allowing a court to exclude anyone, even the accused, if they threatened to disrupt the proceedings. As Danton fumed in prison, all fourteen were condemned to death.

To Camille Desmoulins, the rigged trial was symptomatic of everything that had gone wrong with the revolution. Execution had replaced reason and debate "I shall die in the belief," he wrote to his wife from prison, "that, to make France free, republican and prosperous, a little ink would have sufficed, and only one guillotine."

All fourteen died on April 5, 1794—Germinal 16 in the new calendar. (The plant chosen to signify that day was the lettuce.) Fabre d'Églantine remained theatrical to the last. As the tumbrel carried him to the Place de la Révolution, today's Place de la Concorde, he is said to have scribbled poetry on pieces of paper and thrown them to the crowd.

Another anecdote has him singing "Il pleut, bergère" as he mounted the scaffold, and a third that he lamented the fact that he hadn't finished the poem on which he was working. At this, Danton is supposed to have responded with a pun on the fact that *vers* could mean both "verse" and "worms." "Don't worry," he said. "In a week, you'll have *vers* by the thousands." This story remains dubious, unlike Danton's actual last words, which show his trademark braggadocio surviving to the end. "Hold up my head for everyone to see," he ordered the executioner. "People will expect it."

Had Danton lived, he could have taken bitter satisfaction in the downfall of Robespierre a few months later. By then, the remaining members of the Convention had realized that if as great a man as Danton could be so easily purged, their own lives were even more at risk. Increasingly embattled, Robespierre was repeatedly shouted down in the Convention. When he lost his voice, someone called, "Is it the blood of Danton that chokes you?" Robespierre responded sullenly, "If you wanted Danton, why didn't you vote for him?" It was a question none of those who betrayed their former hero cared to address.

On July 28, as the National Guard arrived to arrest Robespierre and his followers, he tried to shoot himself but only shattered his jaw. A day later, he was guillotined without trial, as he had murdered so many. With its most charismatic figures dead, the revolution lost momentum, faltered, and came to a halt.

❋ ·30· ❋

TAKING THE WATERS

Balmain, Sydney. December 1998. 40°C. As I sit and read, Marie-Dominique swims laps on a rooftop pool. Louise, age eight, matches her stroke for stroke, dipping below her, surfacing ahead, effortless as a seal—being comfortable in her body, an attribute I lacked, was conferred on her at birth.

FOR CENTURIES, THE CITY OF PARIS HAS TRIED TO MAKE SUMMER more bearable for those stranded there. In the 1990s, it spread tons of sand along a stretch of the stone-paved bank of the Seine next to the Pont Neuf. On this *Paris plage* (Paris beach) you could sunbathe, flirt, make sandcastles, dance, drink sodas, eat ice cream—just not swim, since nobody in their right mind would risk going into water described as far back as 1844 as *"sale, troublé, souvent fétide et malsaine"* (dirty, turbid, often foul smelling, and unhealthy.)

Despite this, there were always a few people determined to swim. For them, generations of entrepreneurs have built public pools, or *piscines*. Often little more than half-sunken barges, they offered river water from which at least the larger pieces of debris and most dead animals had been removed. Better filtering had to wait until the mid-1930s, and it only became standard during the Nazi occupation, when German officers, for whom the pools were reserved, demanded it.

Paris's first *piscines* appeared late in the eighteenth century. At one time the Seine supported twenty, of which Piscine Deligny, next to the Place de la Concorde, was the most fashionable. Opened in 1785, it belonged to Barthélémy Turquin, who's also credited with inventing the life jacket. In 1801, his son-in-law took over. A skilled self-promoter who styled himself "*Maître-nageur* Deligny" (master swimmer Deligny), he attached his surname to the until-then-anonymous pool.

In 1840 the Burghs, two enterprising brothers, rebuilt Piscine Deligny. They used timber from the *Dorade*, the steamboat that carried Napoléon's body up the Seine for reburial when it was returned from Saint Helena to Paris that year. Appropriate to such a patron, they surrounded the pool with oriental-style terraces and cafés to create a cigar divan, or Turkish café.

During the Belle Epoque, men-about-town strolled there in the afternoon to smoke and take coffee, but mostly to admire the women in their clinging wool *maillots de bain*. Marcel Proust's mother was among them. He remembered her "splashing and laughing there, blowing him kisses and climbing again ashore, looking so lovely in her dripping rubber helmet, he would not have felt surprised had he been told that he was the son of a goddess."

The Deligny offered private cabins, technically for changing

Piscine Deligny, 1954.

clothes but often misused. One *habitué* reminisced, "American girls learning French at the Alliance Française, just three Metro stops away, would come down to the pool. They seemed to enjoy perfecting their French with me. Sometimes I would take the girls into my cabin to continue their French lessons. It was charming, if not altogether comfortable."

By the 1980s the Deligny was showing its age, and the clientele, in line with venues like the Astoria Baths in New York City, had become almost entirely gay. Its borrowed time ran out in August 1993 when, ignominiously and mysteriously, the ancient construction broke up one night, its rotted timbers settling to the mud of the Seine in what was probably the first example of a swimming pool destroyed by sinking.

A new generation of pools had already supplanted the old wooden establishments. Its star was Piscine Molitor, a landlocked complex that opened in 1929. Olympic champion Johnny Weissmuller hosted the premiere, trained there, and acted as honorary lifeguard until Hollywood recruited him to play Tarzan.

To Parisians, few of whom even had bathrooms, Piscine Molitor offered a taste of luxury. Designed in art deco style, it echoed the liners then plowing the Atlantic. Inside, it was easy to believe one was on the high seas. The city disappeared behind walls of changing cabins topped by cafés, sports shops, hairdressers, and an esplanade that supplanted the terrace of the Deligny as a pickup spot.

In winter a retractable roof covered the space, and the water was frozen for ice skating. At other times it hosted fashion shows and beauty contests. In 1946, swimwear designer Louis Réard chose it to unveil the abbreviated two-piece swimsuit he named the "Bikini," after the Pacific atoll where atomic weapons were tested. When every reputable mannequin refused to model the outfit—small enough, Réard boasted, to fit in a matchbox—he hired showgirl Micheline Bernardini, wife of entrepreneur Alain Bernardin, who would, shortly after, launch what became the city's most famous erotic cabaret, the Crazy Horse Saloon.

Homework at Piscine Molitor, 1966.

After years in decline, the Molitor was modernized in the early twenty-first century. It was incorporated into a hotel complex sufficiently chic to provide a location for the film *Life of Pi*, although critics complained that doors that once opened onto invitingly intimate changing rooms now hid only blank concrete.

A few other public pools survive, including a floating creation in fiberglass in the thirteenth arrondissement, named, improbably, for dancer/singer Josephine Baker. Not notably aquatic, she may never even have set foot in such an unfashionable district, far from the clubs and cabarets of Montmartre.

The city has persevered in trying to create a more permanent

Micheline Bernardini and the first bikini, small enough to fit in a matchbox.

and accessible space for swimming. In 2016 it dredged a stretch of the Canal Saint-Martin, along which barges used to haul goods into the city. Some hundreds of rusty bicycles later, plus a few handguns and copious quantities of drug paraphernalia, this improvised lido opened—only to close almost immediately.

Oliver Gee, an Australian journalist friend, covered the cleanup. I asked him if he knew why the project failed.

"Well, I have an idea . . ."

It took some time to coax out the story, but it was worth the effort.

Following up on a rumor that hinted the canal harbored some

living inhabitants—specifically, a large beaver—Oliver approached an elderly lady sitting by the water and asked if she'd ever seen such a beast.

"*Un castor?*" She shook her head. "No, not a *castor . . .*"

"Are you suggesting some other animal?" he prompted.

(As he told me later, "I thought, you know, maybe rats. Even an otter. But not what came next.")

"The only animals I'm certain lived here," she continued, "are crocodiles."

"Crocodiles?" Oliver said, startled. "How would crocodiles get into the Canal Saint-Martin?"

She lowered her eyes in embarrassment. "I put them there."

Hearing this, I couldn't help being skeptical. In New York, perhaps, but *Paris?*

The existence of alligators and crocodiles under Manhattan was an urban myth of the 1980s. People who'd bought such animals as pets were alarmed when they became large enough to cast thoughtful glances at the family Chihuahua, if not the children. They dumped them down the nearest toilet or storm drain, from where they reached the sewers and thrived.

Oliver had been just as skeptical. With commendable journalistic zeal, he pursued the story, pressing the lady on where she got the animals (from sanitation workers, she claimed, who found them under her house in the Marais, Paris's oldest district) and why she dumped them in the canal (they were getting too big and aggressive to be kept as pets.)

"So . . . did you believe her?" I asked.

"Well, yes," Oliver said. "Eventually. Because it's happened before. Have you heard of Eleanore, the crocodile of the Pont Neuf?"

I hadn't, but an internet search brought me up to date. In March 1984, workers cleaning drains near the Pont Neuf, Paris's oldest bridge, alerted the fire service to the presence of a small crocodile in the sewer.

"She measured between two and three feet," said one of the *sapeurs-pompiers* who trapped her. "We used a shovel and brooms to hold her down, then we tied her around the nose to stop her biting."

A marine biologist identified her as a female *Crocodylus niloticus*, or Nile crocodile, and none the worse for her ordeal.

"Is it likely," I asked Marie-Dominique after I found this article, "that a crocodile could live in the Seine near the Pont Neuf?"

"Well, if any animal could, it'd be a crocodile. And," she added thoughtfully, "it *is* right next to the Quai de la Mégisserie."

The pet shops that line that stretch of boulevard running above the river have long been suspected of consigning unsalable animals to the Seine. If it could swallow puppies and kittens that had outgrown their cuteness, why not a crocodile?

The story even has a happy ending. Having been in the papers, the escapee of 1984 became a celebrity and could not be allowed to disappear. At Vannes, along the Atlantic coast of Brittany, an aquarium adopted her and christened her Eleanore.

Today, ten feet long and weighing more than five hundred pounds, she luxuriates in her own ocean-side condo. It replicates in gray cement the corner of *les égouts* where she was captured, complete with a traditional blue enamel plaque identifying her address as Pont Neuf. Elements of a sewer worker's outfit hang on the wall, though visitors willing to put on the helmet and boots to pay her a visit are few and far between. This suits Eleanore. Like most stars, she values her privacy.

Now, crossing the Pont Neuf, I occasionally pause and look down into the roiling water, alert for the glint of a saurian eye, the flick of a scaly tail. If I needed another excuse not to swim in the Seine, memories of Eleanore would serve very well.

✳ · 31 · ✳

ENTER NAPOLÉON

Tuileries Palace, Paris. December 1804. Court jeweler Martin-Guillaume Biennais places the wreath of fifty solid-gold laurel leaves on the balding head of Europe's most powerful ruler. Napoléon frowns and glances upward, as if to see the object encircling his forehead. "Too heavy." "But, Your Imperial Highness . . ." "I said, 'Too heavy!'" Back in his workshop, Biennais snips off six leaves. They remind him of his six daughters, each in need of a dowry if she's to marry well. Hmmm . . .

IN DOING AWAY WITH THE CHURCH, THE REVOLUTION ALSO DIS-carded the ceremonies that offered consolation to those left to mourn. Piled into carts, the corpses of the guillotined were taken by night to any place where pits existed large enough to accommodate them. Existing cemeteries such as the Madeleine were soon overwhelmed. The bodies of those imprisoned at the convent of Picpus were buried in mass graves dug on its grounds. Others were dumped in an ancient opencast gypsum mine, later to become the Cimetière de Montmartre.

A new cemetery, the Cimetière des Errancis, or "cemetery of the wandering," was hurriedly opened in March 1793. Situated in northern Paris's eighth arrondissement, on what was then the city's outer edge but is near today's Parc Monceau, it is reputed to have displayed over the entrance the sign "Dormir. Enfin!" (To sleep. At last!) Within two years it closed, having absorbed the bodies of 1,119 victims.

Danton, Camille Desmoulins, and Fabre d'Églantine were buried there in April 1794, followed in July by Robespierre and Saint-Just. They were joined by Charles-Gilbert Romme, colorless chairman of the calendar commission. Condemned in May 1795, he committed suicide before he could be guillotined. When an expanding city reached the cemetery in 1848, their skeletons were transferred to the underground ossuary known as the Catacombs, where they lie, unmarked, with thousands of other anonymous dead.

For four years after the death of Robespierre, a five-man committee known as the Directoire, or Directorate, ruled France.

Since the revolution was still technically in progress, the state stuck to Fabre's calendar. Nobody had time to think about revising it. In one of the most corrupt periods in France's history, abstractions took second place to profiteering.

With the young Napoléon Bonaparte as its muscle, the Directoire created satellite states all over Europe and looted them to keep the French economy afloat. If a state couldn't or wouldn't pay the exorbitant taxes demanded, artworks were plundered from its museums and stately homes and sent to augment the Louvre's collection.

Outside France, the Republican calendar was comprehensively mocked. American president John Quincy Adams called it an "incongruous composition of profound learning and superficial frivolity, of irreligion and morality, of delicate imagination and coarse vulgarity." British poet George Ellis, tongue in cheek, published his suggestion for an English version in which the months would be called Snowy, Flowy, Blowy, Showery, Flowery, Bowery, Hoppy, Croppy, Droppy, Breezy, Sneezy, and Freezy.

In the French countryside, life remained so arduous that Fabre's calendar was simply ignored, though the few who gave it serious thought found plenty to criticize.

Its Paris-centricity, for a start. Language and imagery both were based on the weather its framers saw out their own windows. A southerner like Fabre should have been aware that snow and frost were almost unknown in Provence and along the Riviera. Who in those areas could relate to the wintry imagery of Pluviôse, Frimaire, and Brumaire?

As for Lafitte's illustrations, they bore as little relationship to the women of rural France as the models in a *Sports Illustrated* Swimsuit Issue do to the average woman on any American or British beach.

More important, Fabre and his team, in their urge to make everything new, had ignored the degree to which the Gregorian calendar not only imposed a way of life but also reflected one. Over centuries, the church and those ordinary French men and women who worked on the land had developed a relationship with which, for good or ill, both were comfortable.

The traditional religious feasts may have been dictated by the church, but people welcomed them as an excuse to relieve the monotony of their lives. Celebrating the saint's day of a loved one had become second nature in most families. Wishing them "Happy Manure Monday" wasn't the same. And having to wait nine days for Sunday made the week intolerably long. Some frivolously misinterpreted this rule. Told that every tenth day was now a day of rest, they put down their tools on the new "Sunday" as well as the old one. After numerous complaints, the fifth day of each *décade* was made a half holiday, with work finishing at noon.

Worst of all, those who created the calendar knew nothing of running a farm. The treatment of two autumn feasts, Michaelmas and Martinmas, was a prime illustration.

The Feast of Saint Michael on September 29, known as Michaelmas, loomed large in the French farming year. Traditionally the conclusion of the harvest, it was the day from which all leases were dated and on which land rents were paid and workers hired. It also inaugurated the legal year, marking the beginning of tenure for magistrates and other holders of high office. At one time, the church thought it so important that they declared it a holy day of obligation, on which all Catholics were required to attend mass under pain of mortal sin.

At this time of year, geese, hatched in the spring and fed through the summer and fall, were at their fattest. Rather than keep all of them through the winter, farmers killed one and enjoyed a rare roasted bird, a change from the stews and soups on which they existed the rest of the year. A few birds were kept for Christmas, a cheap substitute for the more exotic and expensive turkey. Any geese not eaten were cooked, cut up, and conserved in their own fat for later use in such winter dishes as the unctuous mixture of white haricot beans, sausage, salted pork, and preserved goose known as cassoulet. Nothing of the bird was wasted. Wing feathers provided quills for writing, and the soft down of the breast made an ideal filling for pillows and quilts.

Michaelmas was also the last day on which blackberries could be picked. By tradition, Lucifer, ejected from heaven, fell onto a blackberry bush and cursed the fruit, making it poisonous. The legend disguised a practical lesson: once they became ripe, the berries, if left unpicked, could develop a poisonous fungus. Also, as they ripened and hung low to the ground, foxes and wild dogs urinated on them to mark their territory. Wise wives picked the berries early and used them to make a Michaelmas pie, mixing the still-tart fruit with sweeter apples and a touch of nutmeg and clove.

The manner in which Michaelmas was observed in Britain and France emphasized even more their national differences. In Britain a pervasive gloom characterized the feast, a contrast to its gaiety in rural France. For British farmworkers who'd failed to win a contract, Michaelmas, as the day on which rents must be paid, could mean a "moonlight flit," the whole family sneaking away by night, carrying their possessions. In 1836, satirist George Cruikshank made this the subject of one of his caricatures.

A family does a moonlight flit on Michaelmas.

Charles Dickens captured some of the desolation in his description of Michaelmas in his 1853 novel, *Bleak House*:

> Fog everywhere. Fog up the river, where it flows among green aits and meadows; fog down the river, where it rolls defiled among the tiers of shipping and the waterside pollutions of a great (and dirty) city. Fog on the Essex marshes, fog on the Kentish heights. Fog creeping into the cabooses of collier-brigs; fog lying out on the yards and hovering in the rigging of great ships; fog drooping on the gunwales of barges and small boats.

The French celebrated the Feast of Saint Martin, Martinmas, on November 11, with even more ceremony than Michaelmas. With the harvest over and the penitential season of Advent looming, it was an opportunity to carouse. Traditionally, Martinmas was also the day on which pigs, fed on kitchen scraps through the summer, were slaughtered and their meat salted down or hung up to air-dry into hams and sausages.

And yet on the new calendar, neither of these important feasts was even mentioned. Were they no longer to be observed? If so, when were pigs to be butchered? A slaughter needed organization: the pig sticker called from the next village; the family rallied to help bleed, skin, and prepare the carcass; others to salt down the joints, cut up smaller pieces of meat for sausage, and drain the blood for *boudin noir.* Surely they weren't suggesting that pigs should be fed through the winter? Both the animal and its owners would starve.

Bureaucrats also complained of the new system. The need to transpose dates between the Republican and Gregorian calendars disrupted official documents and complicated international communications. The London *Times* found Fabre's calendar "productive of endless inconvenience in mercantile transactions, in comparing dates of letters and bills of exchange, and possessing not one advantage in return, as it was not even astronomically just."

It survived through the last days of the Directoire and was still in place on Brumaire 18, Year VIII (November 9, 1799), when Napoléon Bonaparte led the coup d'état that formally ended the revolution.

"In revolution there are two types of people," said Napoléon, "those who make it and those who profit from it." Determined to be part of the second group, he adopted the best ideas of the revolution, including the legal system, renamed the Code Napoléon, and the metric system. He kept Robespierre's plan for a network of schools and academies designed to identify the keenest young minds and train them in science, technology, and management. It would lead to the lycée system and a society more effectively educated than most of the world.

The church was restored as an official institution, though no longer as the state religion. As with those other advances of the revolution retained under the First Empire, it was tolerated so long as it was regulated.

The Concordat that authorized this change took effect from Easter Sunday, Germinal 28, Year X (April 18, 1802). The same law reintroduced the Gregorian calendar, and Sunday became again the official and sole day of rest.

Napoléon was crowned—or rather, crowned himself—emperor of the French on Frimaire 11, Year XIII (December 2, 1804), taking the crown from the hands of the pope's representative and placing it on his own head. It was only when he felt completely in charge of the new state that he abolished the Republican calendar, effective January 1, 1806, returning France to the Gregorian calendar that preceded it. The creation of Fabre d'Églantine had survived a little over twelve years.

32

WATCH IT COME DOWN

Santa Monica, California. August 1988. 2 a.m. 36°C.
Even by the ocean the air lies motionless, subdued by
the heat. The cloying scent of night-blooming jasmine is
everywhere. In the faux-Spanish courtyard of a twenties-
style villa, the tiles of a dried-out fountain crawl in a
pattern of orange and black as ladybugs in their thou-
sands struggle and clamber, drunk on heat and perfume.

THE FRENCH NEVER TOOK SCIENCE FICTION SERIOUSLY, LEAST OF
all in one of its most popular forms, the novel of world destruction.

Not so British writers, who for more than a century have relished laying waste to the world, starting with England's green and
pleasant land itself. Sir Arthur Conan Doyle and H. G. Wells set
dinosaurs and Martian war machines roaming, respectively, in *The
Lost World* and *The War of the Worlds*. In Richard Jefferies's *After
London, or Wild England*, a cataclysmic blizzard leaves the home
counties choked by impenetrable woodland. John Christopher's *The
Death of Grass* took the opposite tack, disposing of mankind by kill-
ing the grains we eat.

John Wyndham, walking with his wife along a country lane at night, saw blackberry canes whipping in the wind and was inspired to invent a race of ambulant homicidal plants in *The Day of the Triffids*. Subsequently, in *The Kraken Wakes* and *The Midwich Cuckoos*, he unleashed submarine monsters and gangs of malevolent superchildren.

But nobody so comprehensively laid waste to Britain as J. G. Ballard. In *The Wind from Nowhere*, a gale destroys every sign of human habitation above ground, only to die away inexplicably as the last building crumbles. He followed with *The Drowned World*, in which global warming returns England (and presumably also France) to the era of the dinosaurs. He imagines London as a swamp, the vegetation and fauna of which are reverting to the Triassic through some unspecified biological process. Mankind has retreated to the Arctic. A few stragglers camp out on the top floor of London's Ritz Hotel but are kept awake by the bark of giant lizards echoing down Piccadilly.

His other books were even more anarchic. *The Drought* imagines a layer of pollution covering the oceans, putting an end to evaporation, clouds, rain, and—inevitably—mankind. In *The Crystal World*, a virus attacks the rain forests, turning them to crystal, then does the same to humans.

Neither Ballard nor his predecessors found an answering voice across the channel. French visionaries saw nothing sinister in nature. Climate, nature, the land and its products were to be embraced, celebrated, loved. Jules Verne, the nation's most famous writer of

Barbarella and the interstellar florist.

scientific fantasy, could not have been more benign. No worlds were destroyed in *Twenty Thousand Leagues Under the Sea*, *Journey to the Center of the Earth*, or *Around the World in Eighty Days*. When in the 1960s France did briefly enter the international fantasy scene, the vehicle of its success was equally lightweight—a comic strip that chronicled the mostly sexual adventures of a forty-first-century heroine, Barbarella.

Like Verne's tales of fantastic voyages, *Barbarella* has a flavor of the traveler's tale and bedtime story, nothing that grown-ups need take seriously. In the first of her adventures, Barbarella hitches a ride across the universe on a spaceship filled with flowers. "Is there a place for me among the roses and wild amaranths?" she inquires of the handsome pilot. A true son of Fabre d'Églantine, he responds courteously, "A seat of honor, beautiful orchid."

Though this national indifference to universal ruin intrigued and puzzled the Francophile James Ballard, the fact that disasters and dystopias should fail to flourish on French soil was no more than the Republican calendar would lead us to expect. A nation that could remake the year in the image of nature—however unsuccessfully—would be the last to enjoy seeing it destroyed. Even Sade, the nihilist's nihilist, only flirted with the concept. "To attack the sun," he mused, "to deprive the universe of it, or to use it to set the world ablaze—these would be crimes indeed!"

Once a year, Ballard spent a few weeks on holiday along the Mediterranean. Occasionally he set stories there, fables that hinted at unexpressed urges toward chaos among exiles crowding the Côte d'Azur and Costa Brava. *Super-Cannes* and *Cocaine Nights* are sleek fantasies of the near future. Half Helmut Newton, half Bill Gates, they take place in gated holiday compounds or research establishments where frustrated technocrats or bored Eurotrash vent their frustrations on the weak, who become sacrifices to their existential frenzy. (The stories have a hidden agenda: in 1964 on a family holiday near Alicante, Ballard's wife, Mary, died within a few hours, victim of a runaway infection and inadequate local medical facilities.)

Ballard also set a series of stories in Vermilion Sands, a generic down-at-heel Mediterranean resort of the future. Its craftspeople, bar owners, and part-time writers spend the off-season sculpting the clouds in flimsy lightweight aircraft or operating poetry machines that spew verse on ribbons of tape that tangle around the empty buildings "like some vivid cerise bougainvillea."

In one story of the series, "Prima Belladonna," a botanist raises "choro-flora" plants that sing. They include "soprano mimosas, azalea trios, mixed coloratura herbaceous from the Santiago Garden Choir," and a giant "Khan-Arachnid orchid" that is half diva, half Venus flytrap. The story is subtly subversive, since Jim Ballard disliked music and owned neither radio nor record player.

Vermilion Sands captures that Mediterranean sense of world destruction which the French shun. When the world ends for France, it will, Ballard suggests, expire in the same manner as his imaginary resort, gently but inexorably declining from an excess of those archetypal Gallic afflictions, cafard and ennui: as T. S. Eliot suggested, "not with a bang but a whimper."

The anarchic impulse articulated by Sade was inherited by André Breton and the surrealists, who revered the marquis and wistfully envied his recklessness. "The purest surrealist act," announced Breton, "is walking into a crowd with a loaded gun and firing into it randomly." Not that anyone in the group ever did anything so ill-mannered. Breton's father, after all, had been a policeman. Their outrages were limited to disrupting theatrical events staged by their rivals or abusing priests or nuns in the street.

To Ballard, France was inseparable from surrealism. In common with many Britons, he saw it as an exotic Continental courtesan with whom he could indulge fantasies that no British partner would countenance. Above his desk he pinned a Max Ernst collage of a nude woman, her head replaced with that of a predatory bird.

Once Steven Spielberg's film adaptation of *Empire of the Sun* made him rich, Ballard commissioned an artist to repaint two canvases by the Belgian surrealist Paul Delvaux that were believed to have been destroyed during World War II. His favorite, *The Mirror*, showed a woman clothed in a formal gown, seated before a mirror that reflects her naked. Ballard never hung the painting. For a time he kept it leaning on the wall next to his desk, ready for that moment when, he once confided, he anticipated it opening like a portal, inviting him to step in.

He talked often about moving to France. "I go to the Côte d'Azur every summer," he said, "and, if I could afford it, would happily live there for the rest of my life." Since his personal fortune at that time exceeded £4 million, it was not money that prevented him. Did he fear that France would free his imagination, and with it his hunger for destruction? Could he see himself as part of an expat mob roaming the streets of Cannes, hunting victims to murder? These were questions only the woman in *The Mirror* could answer.

33

WHO WAS THAT MASKED MAN?

*Downtown Los Angeles. March 1992. 10 p.m.
14°C. Reaching the filming location means thread-
ing through trailers housing makeup and costume
staff. Fat black cables snake from humming genera-
tors toward a blaze of light. A gantry looks down on
a narrow, mirrored club. "What's this movie about,
anyway?" A grip nods toward a stocky figure in
leather jacket and dark glasses waiting impassively
in the shadows. "Him."*

IF NO SCHOLAR HAS DONE SO ALREADY, ONE WILL EVENTUALLY
write a thesis about the French Revolution that claims responsibility
on its behalf for the existence of Batman—not to mention Superman, Wonder Woman, the Lone Ranger, and the Incredible Hulk.
Would there have been Clark Kent or Bruce Wayne without Sir
Percy Blakeney and the Scarlet Pimpernel? Probably not.

Of the numerous novels, plays, and musical works inspired by
the revolution, most sided with its victims. Authors who before 1789
showed French aristocracy as oppressors of the virtuous poor now

took the opposite point of view, celebrating them as sensitive and kindly souls martyred by a bloodthirsty mob.

In *A Tale of Two Cities*, Charles Dickens writes his aristos villainous, none more so than the Marquis St. Evrémonde, who represents the worst excesses of the ancien régime. Having run down a pedestrian, the marquis tosses some money out the window and orders the coachman to drive on. But Dickens is just as critical of the revolution. In Madame Defarge, a *tricoteuse* who sits knitting under the guillotine as her victims die, he created one of the most memorable of all fictional revolutionaries.

The book's moral hero is a disreputable English barrister, Sydney Carton. Drawn into the revolution by chance, he redeems a wasted life by going to the guillotine to console a terrified girl. Dickens's final words for Carton are among his most memorable: "It is a far, far better thing that I do, than I have ever done; it is a far, far better rest that I go to than I have ever known."

The more prolific Baroness Orczy, writing half a century later than Dickens, was not much for shades of character. An aristocrat herself, she fled Hungary as a child to escape a peasant uprising, an experience that made her understandably hostile to rebels. The manner in which she describes the Paris mob at the opening of her first novel about the revolution, *The Scarlet Pimpernel*, leaves no doubt about her sympathies: "A surging, seething, murmuring crowd of beings that are human only in name, for to the eye and ear they seem naught but savage creatures, animated by vile passions and by the lust of vengeance and of hate."

Her hero, no less broadly drawn, is a titled Englishman, Sir Percy Blakeney. Between 1905 and 1940, she published more than a dozen novels and short story collections about his exploits. Blakeney is one of popular fiction's first clandestine heroes. Alexandre Dumas may have beaten Orczy to first place with his 1844 novel about Edmond Dantès, an escaped convict, wrongly convicted, who pursues his revenge in disguise as the fictitious count of Monte Cristo, but only Orczy explored such a character as extensively, furnishing many of the details that we still associate with the hero in hiding.

Before Orczy, few fictional characters hid their expertise. Sherlock Holmes enjoyed demonstrating his skill at deduction and Svengali his ability to hypnotize. But Sir Percy allows everyone, even his wife, to regard him as a wimp and a fop. Only a few confederates know of his efforts to smuggle aristos out of France while evading the malevolent Chauvelin, officer of the Committee of Public Safety. Calling himself the Scarlet Pimpernel, Sir Percy leaves behind a calling card—another trope of the hidden-hero persona—with the image of that tiny star-shaped red flower, *Anagallis arvensis*. He also gleefully circulates the rhyme that became one of the most memorable aspects of the series:

> *We seek him here, we seek him there,*
> *Those Frenchies seek him everywhere.*
> *Is he in heaven?—Is he in hell?*
> *That damned, elusive Pimpernel.*

No later masked hero would be complete without some similar announcement—a costume, slogan, or catchphrase: "It's a bird . . . it's a plane . . ." for Superman, the Lone Ranger's "Hi ho, Silver!," the Shadow's "Who knows what evil lurks in the hearts of men?" As for the Scarlet Pimpernel's nom de guerre, the name of a flower, might the Baroness have been influenced by Fabre and his botanical almanac? On this topic the lady, seldom lost for words, was uncharacteristically silent.

Parisians, having proved in 1789 the value of taking to the streets, did so again in July 1830 and June 1832. The latter uprising lasted only two days, but we know it well because it inspired Victor Hugo's novel *Les Misérables* and the films and musicals that followed. Then there was the brief anarchist rebellion of 1871 known as the Commune: in the power vacuum following the siege of Paris by the armies of Prussia, the citizens of Montmartre—the most militantly socialist of all Paris districts—declared the city free of all government except that of its people.

As the French army sat in barracks and the administration dithered in Bordeaux, on the other side of the country, the Communards confiscated all church property and ended religious teaching in schools. Rents were suspended, and pawnshops forced to return household goods and tools pledged by starving families. Workers were encouraged to take over businesses whose owners had fled the city. The families of National Guard members killed fighting the

Prussians were promised pensions, a provision that, had it ever been introduced, would have extended to both unmarried companions and illegitimate children.

Though Fabre d'Églantine had taken little interest in the ideals of the revolution, he shared in its immortality at least by proxy, particularly during this episode, since the Commune also decided to restore the Republican calendar. But before it could do so, it collapsed. Guided by traitors who led them through the old gypsum mines that honeycomb Montmartre, soldiers from outside Paris with no allegiance to the rebels brutally suppressed the uprising. Thousands died or were exiled to New Caledonia.

The readiness of the Communards to revive the Republican calendar suggests that Fabre and his collaborators were on the right track in attempting to shake loose the naming and counting of days from church control.

In 1849, Auguste Comte, French philosopher and proponent of positivism, had proposed a solar calendar with thirteen months of twenty-eight days each. An additional festival day, commemorating the dead, made up the total of 365. Following Fabre's lead, Comte renumbered the years, beginning with the "great crisis" of 1789. Months and days were named for great figures in science, religion, philosophy, industry, and literature, ranging from Gutenberg and Shakespeare to Buddha and Socrates. In total his calendar honored 558 individuals, including a few villains (among them Napoléon), whose name days would be devoted to their "perpetual execration."

Comte's proposal failed to find a following, but the calendar—

unlike the weather—remained a problem about which people continued to *do* something, though not with much success. In 1929 Soviet Russia abolished Sunday in favor of a rest day taken at some more convenient time during the week, but returned to the traditional week in 1940. Among other attempts to streamline the ordering of the year, only the introduction of daylight saving time has achieved anything like international acceptance. Sunday remains the international day of rest, and at least in France, children continue to be named for the same "beatified skeletons pulled from the catacombs of Rome." Efficiency and rationality have proved nowhere a match for the weight of custom.

34

NIGHT OF THE SCYTHE

*Théâtre du Châtelet, Paris. June 6, 1911. 10 p.m.
28°C. Vaslav Nijinsky dances the Paris premiere of* Le
Spectre de la rose, *concluding with his heart-stopping
leap through an open window. On the other side, four
young members of the city's gay elite, among them Jean
Cocteau, wait to catch him in midair. Wrapped in warm
towels, he's carried, exhausted, to a bath filled with
warm water, where they peel off his skintight costume
and sponge the sweat from his shivering naked body.*

IT MAY BE ONLY IN FRANCE THAT THE ARRIVAL OF SPRING FAILS TO
excite the most exuberant emotions.

Italian music soars in praise of warmth's return and the re-
affirmation of life, and Russian novels ring with ecstatic evocations
of that moment when the rivers thaw and begin again to flow. In
Tolstoy's *War and Peace*, Andrei Bolkonsky sees his ruined life sym-
bolized in an apparently dead oak. Passing again in spring, he finds
the tree in vigorous full leaf and is seized by "a causeless springtime
feeling of joy and renewal."

Anyone who studies English literature beyond fifth grade will eventually encounter William Chaucer's *The Canterbury Tales* and its celebration of April, which "with its sweet-smelling shower has pierced the drought of March to the root."

Even American students unfamiliar with fourteenth-century English verse welcome April as the month of spring break, and the start of the season of wet T-shirts and beer pong.

Not so France. To the French, March and April are too early to celebrate a year that's hardly begun. These are the months to get one's head down, to work long hours and concentrate on the golden days of July and August, the *vacances*, when one can mellow back and truly appreciate the sensual possibilities of the greatest country in the world.

Fabre d'Églantine seems to have sensed this in his bones. Why else would he have chosen poisonous hemlock, a knife, and the Judas tree to signify Germinal, the month that began on the former March 21 and ran to April 19? They imply apprehension, distaste, and a recognition that so fundamental a disturbance in nature must have a price.

One could almost believe that Fabre was present in spirit at the Théâtre des Champs-Élysées on the night of May 29, 1913, for the premiere of a new ballet by the Ballets Russes of Sergei Diaghilev, *Le Sacre du printemps* (*The Rite of Spring*), to music by Igor Stravinsky. It would have been day 10 of Prairial in the new calendar, and the emblematic object, appropriately, was the *faux*, or "scythe."

The Paris appearances of the Ballets Russes reflected the respect

Jean Cocteau's impression of Igor Stravinsky composing The Rite of Spring.

for seasons that dominated French theater, art, and fashion. Diaghilev developed ballets to a peak of refinement, then unveiled them in seasons of three or four productions. After playing them in repertory in Paris for a few weeks, they moved on to Rome or London, riding, it was hoped, a wave of exuberant reviews and leaving behind an audience more eager than ever for the company's return.

Aware of the shock effect of his ballets, Diaghilev strove to maximize it. When Jean Cocteau asked what it would take to have him commission a ballet, the impresario simply said, "Astonish me."

As he readied the 1913 season, Paris was still digesting the stylistic advances of 1909, when the gorgeous costumes and decor of Léon Bakst and Alexandre Benois, the music of Borodin and Rimsky-Korsakov, and, above all, the dancing and choreography of Vaslav Nijinsky had ripped through the artistic community in a shrapnel of new ideas that transformed fashion, music, and design.

The year 1910 brought a startling version of Debussy's *L'Après-midi d'un faune*, for which Nijinsky both conceived the choreography and danced the role of a satyr, half man, half goat. Mirroring the two-dimensional decorations on Greek vases, he acted out an erotic encounter with some nymphs, at the climax of which he lay facedown on a scarf one had left behind and masturbated.

Nijinsky again dominated the 1911 season with *Le Spectre de la rose*. A dreaming girl conjures up her vision of erotic desire, the embodiment of a rose. When she has been excited to the peak of ecstasy, the spirit launches itself weightlessly through a window, apparently to disperse on the evening air.

For 1913, Diaghilev needed something even more innovative. Listening to Stravinsky hammer out a piano version of *The Rite of Spring*, subtitled *Pictures from Pagan Russia in Two Parts*, he wasn't sure he'd found it.

Stravinsky imagined a tribe fearful that the spring, on which their survival depended, would fail to thaw the ice and germinate the grain. To ingratiate themselves with the spirits, they sacrifice a young woman who, at the climax of the ritual, dances herself to death.

"Does it go on like this much longer?" Diaghilev asked, wincing at the pounding, repetitive chords, for all the world like the chugging of a giant engine—or, as Stravinsky intended, the stamping of feet in a primitive dance.

Without stopping, Stravinsky snarled, "Only to the end," and thundered on.

Diaghilev faced a complex decision in which his liking, or otherwise, for the music was only one factor. More showman than aesthete, he thought less about the worth of Stravinsky's score than about how to fill the enormous new Théâtre des Champs-Élysées.

He was impatient with his regular choreographer, Michel Fokine, and mindful that Nijinsky, who had replaced Fokine as his lover, was eager to develop his choreographic ideas. But Nijinsky's inventiveness was not matched with diplomacy. Inarticulate and unable to reason with dancers, he bullied them to the point of breakdown.

Diaghilev's dilemma was classically Parisian. Should he lead with another crowd-pleaser like *Scheherazade* or *Le Spectre de la rose* that would wring coos of delight from the rich patrons who took a box for the season? Or with an unknown work almost certain to enrage them? Shrewdly, he decided on the latter and gave Nijinsky his head. Long-term success lay, he reasoned, with a *succès de scandale* that would sustain his reputation for innovation.

As *Le Sacre du printemps* had no male lead role for him to dance, Nijinsky poured his imagination and incipient schizophrenia into the choreography. Zelda Fitzgerald, another schizophrenic seized with an urge to dance, described the distorted perceptions that sometimes accompany an attack. "I see odd things," she wrote. "People's arms too long, or their faces as if they were stuffed and they look tiny and far away, or suddenly out of proportion." One sees a similar effect in the shapeless flannel costumes of *Le Sacre du printemps*, the fright wigs and comic bonnets worn by the peasants, the stamping and spasming of the steps, and the frenzy with which the sacrificial maiden dances to her death.

That the ballet would be greeted with hostility was a foregone conclusion. No opera house, the Théâtre des Champs-Élysées had plenty of cheap seats to accommodate spectators eager for sensation. Some were so ready to disrupt the show that they brought whistles, which they began blowing even before the curtain rose.

Diaghilev gambled that the scandal of that first night would take on a life of its own more durable than the ballet itself, and guarantee full houses for the rest of the season. In 1925 the producers of *Revue Nègre*, also using the Théâtre des Champs-Élysées, would follow his lead, restructuring what had been a relatively staid show to feature a near-naked Josephine Baker doing her goofy version of the Charleston.

To maximize the furor, Diaghilev staged the ballet only twice in Paris and three times in London during that first season, and then shelved it, knowing that speculation and exaggeration would garner far more *réclame* for the company than any amount of advertising. He wasn't disappointed. "In Paris in 1923," he wrote, "I was accosted, as ever, by Gertrude Stein."

"Ten years, Mr. Diaghilev," she said. "Can you believe it?"

"Since what, Miss Stein?"

"Since that extraordinary night."

"I wasn't aware that you were there," I said.

"Of course I was there!"

Then she sighed and said, "Ah, Nijinsky."

He played the same card in 1917 with *Parade*. To stage, in the darkest moments of the war, a ballet about the circus, designed by Picasso and choreographed by Fokine, with music played on bottles partly filled with water, was seen by many as callous trivialization, but Diaghilev threw more fuel on the fire by handing out free tickets to soldiers on leave and to the rowdiest bohemians in Montparnasse. He also encouraged Fokine to use elements of African-American dance in his choreography, specifically the one-step, described by Harlem Hellfighters bandleader James Reese Europe as "the national dance of the Negro."

Attending the first performance, young composer Francis Poulenc was as shocked as the rest of the audience: "A one-step is danced in *Parade*! When *that* began, the audience let loose with boos and applause. For the first time, music hall was invading Art-with-a-capital-A." Women tried to blind librettist Jean Cocteau with hatpins, and for subsequent performances sensualists hired boxes in order to fornicate during the uproar. Having correctly judged the French appetite for the roller-coaster sensations of seasonality, the great impresario must have been more than content.

35

ONE PERFECT ROSE

Versailles, Île-de-France. 1715. Louis XIV, believing that bathing removes a protective layer that keeps out disease, has washed only three times in his life. Instead, the scent of roses permeates the newly built palace. Visitors are sprayed with rose water, with which the king also douses his shirts. In each room rose petals float in bowls of water, and courtesans anoint themselves with rose oil, each gram of which uses thirty kilos of flowers.

More so in France than anywhere else in the world, political survival turns on a gesture.

Its rulers have traditionally displayed a flair for shows and symbols. Versailles under Louis XIV was as gaudy as Las Vegas. Lavish banquets concluded with musical shows that tested the inventiveness of the most skilled designers and performers. That the king himself danced in such performances added to his stature.

The revolutionaries of 1789 showed they had learned this lesson. When they burst into the Bastille on July 14, the ancient prison held only seven inmates, and the rebels were less interested in releasing them than in seizing the weapons stored there. But the symbolism of destroying the ancient fortress made such details superfluous.

In August 1944, Charles de Gaulle led a triumphant walk down the Champs-Élysées to signify the liberation of the city from German occupation. Since June 1940 he had directed a Free French government from exile in suburban London, but the Allies approaching Paris agreed to hang back until he made his lap of victory. It guaranteed his place at the center of national power for the next twenty-five years.

The posters, barricades, and manifestos of student uprising of May 1968 also proved more theater than politics, but as historians downgraded it from revolution to mere *événements*—"events"—politicians took note of its most important lesson: power would increasingly belong to those who could entertain as well as persuade.

By the time de Gaulle surrendered the presidency in 1969 after ten years in office, younger voters were weary of his stiff, lofty style of government. They wanted a head of state both powerful and human, someone whose hand they might even shake—who could, as Rudyard Kipling urged in his poem "If—," "talk with crowds and keep your virtue / Or walk with Kings—nor lose the common touch."

No modern French politician was a more skillful showman than François Mitterrand, who would serve as president from 1981 to 1995, the longest term of any to hold the office. To counter de

Gaulle's history as wartime leader, Mitterrand traded on his experience in the Resistance. Each year, he led a pilgrimage to the summit of a rocky outcrop in Burgundy known as la Roche du Solutré. Associated with pilgrims since the Middle Ages, the rock had special significance for Mitterrand: he'd hidden from the Germans nearby.

Once he became president and began inviting colleagues and allies to join him and his family and friends in the climb, the press took a keen interest in the guest list. Each year's walk—evoking Mitterrand's links to the war, nature, and the national heritage—and those who made it with him became news.

The most significant publicity gesture of Mitterrand's period in office, however, took place on the day of his inauguration in May 1981 and hinged on a superficially insignificant prop: a single red rose.

Although its national flower is the iris, France has always accorded a special position of honor for the rose. During the Middle Ages, Guillaume de Lorris's allegorical poem "Roman de la rose" ("The Romance of the Rose") was popular all over Europe. A young man dreams of entering the walled garden surrounding the Fountain of Narcissus in hopes of stealing a rose. Pierced instead with arrows by Love, he flees, doomed to yearn for the bloom he cannot possess.

The rose became the symbol of love, the bud signifying virginity, the full-blown blossom standing for the woman open to every erotic experience, and the thorns the pain of unrequited or unfulfilled love. In time, the single rose as a token of love declined into a cliché, mocked by Dorothy Parker:

> *Why is it no one ever sent me yet*
> *One perfect limousine, do you suppose?*
> *Ah no, it's always just my luck to get*
> *One perfect rose.*

The scent of roses suffused the court of Louis XIV, earning it the name "the Perfumed Court." Marie Antoinette was often painted holding a rose. When Fabre d'Églantine added the name of a rose to his own, he reaffirmed the flower's importance in the intellectual life of France.

In modern times, the new president of the Republic traditionally begins his first day in office by laying a wreath on the tomb of the unknown soldier. In the afternoon, the mayor of Paris hosts a formal reception in his honor at the town hall.

In 1981, Mitterrand broke with protocol. Following the mayoral reception, he didn't, as was customary, go directly to the presidential palace, the Élysée. Instead, his motorcade crossed the river and climbed the hill of Montagne Sainte-Geneviève to the Panthéon, where the great of France are interred. Leaving the car a block away, he walked alone to the building through jubilant crowds, carrying the symbol of his Socialist Party, a long-stemmed red rose.

As he approached the building's columned façade, the crowd fell back, leaving him to climb the steps alone (though shadowed by a surreptitious TV team). As he did so, conductor Daniel Barenboim, on the far side of the square, lifted his baton to lead the Orchestre de Paris in the last movement of Beethoven's Ninth Symphony.

Millions of viewers watched live as Mitterrand crossed the empty floor of the Panthéon (Foucault's pendulum was taken down for the occasion), paused before its monuments, and descended to the crypt. Striding confidently along its anonymous corridors, he laid roses on the tombs of Jean Moulin, leader of the resistance; socialist pioneer Jean Jaurès; and Victor Schoelcher, who campaigned for the abolition of slavery.

As he stepped out again into the open air, the symphony reached its climax in the famous "Ode to Joy," which is also, significantly, the anthem of the European Union. Light rain began to fall, but Mitterrand spurned offers of an umbrella, remaining in the open until the music reached its triumphant conclusion: the man of power, respectful of nature and art.

Behind this apparently unrehearsed event lay weeks of planning by an informal committee of media advisers, including Roger Hanin, Mitterrand's movie-star brother-in-law; TV producer Serge Moati, a specialist in news broadcasts; Jack Lang, his young minister of culture; and historian Claude Manceron.

Manceron, an unlikely recruit to this chic and trendy crew, was then in his late fifties, with a wild white beard spilling halfway down his chest. A childhood victim of polio, he was confined to a wheelchair. His sense of history was acute: it was he who urged Mitterrand to embrace the nation's oldest traditions and the symbolism of the rose.

François Mitterrand at the Panthéon, 1981.

Inside the Panthéon, assistants had been strategically placed behind pillars, ready to point him down the correct passages and hand him fresh roses as required. But the millions who watched on television saw only a president who needed no retinue, who knew exactly where he was going but maintained at the same time a decent humility and reverence for tradition.

36

THE DARLING BUDS OF MAY

Grasse, Alpes-Maritimes. August 2017. 4 p.m. 18°C.
Perfume seems to suffuse the air of this hillside town,
the heart of the fragrance industry. The headquarters of
parfumiers Fragonard fills a four-story building that
drops down a steep hillside from the street. Entering at
the top floor, one descends past a museum of perfume
into a retail area whose vendeuses swim in a miasma
of rose, jasmine, vanilla, cedar, and orange blossom.
Perfume must permeate their flesh like a marinade.
Lucky the lover who welcomes such a living bouquet
to his bed.

FABRE D'ÉGLANTINE WAS BARELY IN HIS GRAVE WHEN BLIGHT FELL
on his vision of a metropolitan France ruled in accordance with
nature and the seasons.

Its centerpiece had been Floréal, the second month of spring,
beginning on April 20 and ending on May 19. As the flower to signify its first day he naturally chose the rose, emblem of his own er-
ratic career.

In doing so, he betrayed an ignorance of botany. Few roses bloom so early in the year, nor survive the often blustery weather. As Shakespeare wrote, "Rough winds do shake the darling buds of May." The season is more appropriately celebrated by Floréal 7, our April 26, a day when traditionally one presents a posy of the modest muguet, or lily of the valley, to a loved one. Sellers with baskets of the flower appear on street corners across France, encouraged by a long-standing convention that any money they make is tax-free.

When Louis Lafitte painted the image representing Floréal for the illustrated edition of the Republican calendar, he knew better than to include a rose. Instead he framed his demure brunette with muguet and another early bloomer, lilac.

His painting is more fashion plate than pinup. The model's white dress, in the so-called Empire style, falls in soft folds from a band under her breasts. It recalls the shepherdess chemise dress so scandalously worn by Juliette Récamier in the famous painting by Jacques-Louis David.

To promote Paris as the capital of a new world state as mighty as Greece or Rome, Madame Récamier posed reclining in a faux-Roman interior, wearing a gown similar to the one shown by Lafitte but with her feet shockingly bare. To Britons, these filmy, semi-transparent gowns, equivalents of the modern nightdress, were yet more evidence of France's depravity.

For all the promise of green shoots pushing out of the ground and babies, conceived in the long winter nights, fidgeting to be born, as many factors in May hint at disasters to come. T. S. Eliot would stigmatize April as "the cruellest month," but May is the better candidate, particularly as far as France is concerned. Historically, politically, culturally, agriculturally, May has traditionally meant bad news.

For those on the land, May was filled with foreboding. What if grain stored since the harvest had become damp and spoiled, as happened in 1787? What if the weather brought hail, a late frost, even a hurricane? Would the young crops survive?

Many seeds that germinate in May are social rather than agricultural. They betray a sense of the month as troubled, portentous with hints of incipient violence. Communists and socialists celebrate May 1, May Day, as a workers' holiday, a pretext for protests and demonstrations. It has also historically been the month when armies come back to life and old conflicts are reaffirmed. Officers shake out their uniforms and load their weapons, ready to march when the ground thaws. Wives and lovers are sent back to the kitchen. "Silken dalliance in the wardrobe lies," wrote Shakespeare in *Henry V*. "Now thrive the armourers."

A recital of French disasters that took place in May makes sobering reading:

In May 1789 the peasantry and middle class first demanded a voice in government. By July, France was in flames.

In May 1815 Napoléon, having escaped from Elba, raged across Europe in a rampage that ended at Waterloo in June. In May 1821, he would die in exile on Saint Helena.

In May 1871 mass slaughter ended the brief anarchist uprising known as the Paris Commune.

And in May 1968 the students of Paris erupted into the streets.

Would these events have taken place in August or November? Almost certainly not. In May, the blood is hot. Testosterone is in the air. But as the season changes, so does the resolve. Napoléon's return lasted a mere hundred days, the Commune only twenty-eight. The *événements de '68* began on May 3 but petered out by June 23.

In the half century following the death of Napoléon, liberty, equality, and fraternity were eclipsed by wine, women, and song. Paris became the courtesan of Europe. To illustrate the month of Floréal in a calendar published in the 1880s, the artist Lucien Métivet showed two dandies bantering with a couple of flower girls selling much more than violets. In another almanac image of 1896, a pretty Jacobin shows shapely ankles as she pounds a revolutionary drum.

Even after the Republican calendar was discontinued, echoes remained. Political commentators used the old names for the months to remind those listening of what the English call "the bad old days" and modern Germans, in speaking of the Nazi era, call "in früheren Zeiten" (former times). Historians refer to the coup d'état that brought Napoléon to power by its Republican date, Brumaire 18, Year VIII (November 9, 1799), while because Robespierre was overthrown on Thermidor 9 of Year II (July 27, 1794), any such upheaval within a revolution is called a Thermidorean reaction and its prime movers Thermidoreans.

Yet "Thermidor" survives today mainly as a culinary term. In

1896, chef Auguste Escoffier was in charge of the kitchen at Maison Maire, a restaurant near the newly opened Théâtre de la Porte Saint-Martin in Paris. Among his signature dishes was a concoction of lobster in a cream-and-cognac sauce. Since the theater had recently had a success with a revival of Victorien Sardou's play *Thermidor*, about the fall of Robespierre, Escoffier renamed the dish lobster thermidor in its honor.

The almanac format could be adapted to even less creditable ends. In 1929 the Paris surrealists, in order to raise money for their embattled Dadaist colleagues in Brussels, published an erotic almanac. Called simply *1929*, it included salacious poetry by André Breton, Benjamin Péret, and Louis Aragon and was illustrated with four photographs by Man Ray. They show an anonymous but still recognizable Ray and his companion Alice Prin, aka Kiki, engaged in sexual intercourse. Almost all the copies were seized by French Customs, making this one of the most sought-after surrealist items.

And Fabre d'Églantine? He wasn't entirely erased from history. In 1888 Paris assigned him at least a toehold on immortality. A street in the twelfth arrondissement, near the Picpus convent where so many victims of the Terror lie buried, was named in his honor.

37

GLEANERS

*Bermondsey, London SE1. February 1978. 4 a.m.
8°C. From midnight, the ancient square fills with tac-
iturn men unloading the contents of unmarked vans
onto the paving slabs that give the market its name, the
Stones. Hissing pressure lamps shed blue-white light
on silver pitchers and crystal wineglasses. Other men
squat furtively against the walls next to a few mono-
grammed knives and forks, frayed scraps of Elizabe-
than embroidery, a saucerless Georgian coffee cup: not
so much stock as loot.*

FOR A SMALL BUT DETERMINED GROUP OF PARISIANS, MAY DAY IS
mainly interesting as the start of the season for the secondhand street
markets known as *brocantes*.

Frustrated after having been penned inside during the winter
months, sellers, both amateur and professional, load the contents of
attics or garages into their vans and head for the streets and squares
designated by local councils as sites for sales.

They've been doing so for centuries. Only the terminology

changes. These days, a health-conscious society less accommodating of vermin shuns the term *marché aux puces* (flea market). They prefer *vide-grenier* (literally "attic emptier"), *grand balai* (big sweep-out), or *marché pour tous* (market for everyone), but most use the all-purpose term *brocante*. In the trade, sellers identify themselves with the old term for rag picking, *chineur*.

Serious *chineurs* avoid any event using the words *antiquaire* or *antique*. *Antiquaires*, rating themselves above mere *brocanteurs*, hope to attract the carriage trade. Some erect tentlike canvas pavilions and fit them out like shops. Brewing some coffee, they seat themselves at a Louis XVI desk of dubious provenance, and open *Le Monde*. Despite this impression of indifference, they are as alert as any spider to the punter who strays close to their web. In an instant they're at their side, inviting them to "just *feel* that embroidery, all original, I assure you. And try this chair. What princes, even kings, have sat here? American Express? *Naturellement, monsieur*. And of *course* we can ship it to South Dakota."

The first temperate weekend of the year sang the same siren song to me as to the *chineurs* of Paris. Of the five or six serious *brocantes* (those with two hundred sellers or more) scattered across the city, the most promising was in the fourteenth arrondissement. The farthest south of Paris districts, jammed between Montparnasse and the Périphérique, it combines nineteenth-century workers' housing with light industry and the characterless high-rise blocks of rent-controlled apartments known as HLMs: *habitation à loyer modéré*.

When I arrived, about a hundred trestle tables had colonized

Paris brocante, *or junk market.*

a small square and a few side streets. Sellers, bundled up against a wind that still carried an edge of winter, sat behind them, hands shoved in pockets, wearing the expression of slightly pained boredom that comes with the territory.

Unlike *antiquaires*, *chineurs* don't encourage you to buy. If anything, they imply that you are an unwelcome interruption to their day. If you hold up an object and inquire, "Combien?" they will stare at it as if they've never seen it before, then shrug and mumble an amount, often turning their back as they do so, a classic gesture of "take it or leave it" that has one reaching guiltily for one's wallet.

I was shuffling through a pile of the 1930s picture magazine *Vu*, hoping to find one with a cover by Man Ray, when someone called my name from the opposite side of the alley.

"Might have known you'd be here," said Harry Callaghan, holding out a meaty paw enclosed in a fingerless mitten knitted from gray wool.

Harry was that rarity, an Anglo *chineur*. From his accent I'd guess East Coast USA, but it was so overlaid with the residue of places he'd lived and worked that the original was lost forever. He was probably tall, but years of browsing, hands in pockets, through junk markets and squatting to rummage in cardboard boxes half-hidden under competitors' stalls had given him a permanent slouch.

His white beard blended with a mop of gray hair, neither trimmed since the Reagan administration, if then. Both exploded like stuffing from a gutted mattress, topped by a large felt hat he kept permanently jammed just above his ears.

"I never thought I'd see you go retail," I said, glancing at his table.

For Harry to set up shop, even one so temporary as this *brocante* stall, was as unexpected as finding a peacock roosting on your back fence. I knew him only as what's called a "runner" or "scout." Finding a salable item, these freelancers agree on a price with the dealer and sell it on immediately.

He looked uncomfortable. "Yeah . . . well . . . you know . . . Stuff was piling up, and the old lady . . ."

I looked around. "Clytie not here?"

Harry's consort was about twenty years younger than him, and certainly prettier. Allowing for the feral expression that comes with the *brocante* life, she could have passed for Leslie Caron's younger sister. Having been christened Clytemnestra made her a street fighter since kindergarten. Each time we met, I remembered the advice of one Virginian about a Southern lady of his acquaintance. "Lay a hand on her," he warned, "and you'll draw back a bloody stump."

"No," Harry said. "Sunday. Lunch with the *marraine*. Marie-Dominique with you?"

I shook my head. "Same thing." Sunday lunch with mother, godmother, grandmother, or favorite aunt was a ritual hardwired into French female DNA.

"So . . . what are you working on?" he asked.

I told him. Somewhere inside that jungle of hair, eyes lit up.

"Ah. I might have something for you."

Rummaging under his table, he dragged out a cardboard carton and made room for it on the table.

"Got this in a house sale the other day. Haven't had a chance to go through it."

Something as heavy as a brick thudded onto his table. Roughly cubic, cut from pale gray stone, it measured about twelve centimeters on each side. I recognized a cobblestone, identical with the millions paving French streets.

"Guaranteed to have been used in '68," he said. "Imagine getting one of those up the back of your head."

I hefted it. Some stones weighed three or four kilos. This one belonged to the smaller variety and tipped the scales at about a kilo. Still more than enough to give someone a nasty headache. Some unlucky members of the police and militia at whom they were flung in May 1968 suffered shattered limbs and fractured skulls.

May '68 made the paving stone a signature object, as emblematic as Marianne's Phrygian cap in 1789. The first students to dig up the stones were surprised to find they weren't cemented, just bedded loose in an inch of sand to allow a little play when traffic passed over. The sand provided just that edge of fantasy that stimulated creativity. Overnight, a new graffito appeared on the walls of Paris: "Sous le pavé, la plage" (under the paving, there's a beach).

Harry hefted the stone. "What do you reckon it's worth?"

"Why should it be worth anything?" I said. "You can pick them up anyplace they're mending the roads."

"Yeah, that's you. What about someone in . . ." He gave a wave that encompassed everything from the next arrondissement to outer Mongolia.

"No idea." I looked at the carton. "Anything else in there?"

He rummaged deeper, unearthing yellowing copies of *Le Figaro* and *Le Soir* with photographs of baton charges and burning cars. There were faded manifestos forecasting the demise of democracy in general and General de Gaulle in particular, preceded by that of the police, the universities, the Ministry of Culture, the church, the press, and God, that had been run off on office duplicators normally used for school circulars and lunch menus. But all revolutions are by their nature amateur, made up as the principals go along.

Australia had never experienced a revolution. Everything came easily to "the lucky country," as we complacently called it. But I could remember the racing of the blood that came with reading of internal strife in other cultures.

1789 . . . 1871 . . . 1968 . . . Revolutions were like the seasons. Always another one along in a minute, with each upheaval igniting the same passions. The issues changed, but not the rhetoric, nor the wardrobe. The crowds harangued by Danton in his red surcoat shared the elation of those listening to Louise Michel, the "Red Virgin" of the Commune, and that of the students in May 1968 who gathered in the Théâtre de l'Odéon to cheer a carrot-topped rabble-rouser named Daniel Cohn-Bendit, aka "Danny the Red."

"Ah, here's something."

From the carton, Harry took a tattered, rolled poster. A stark and bloodstained face glared at me, surrounded by a message in block capitals: "Bourgeois. Vous n'Avez Rien Compris" (Middle class, you have understood nothing). As if the students understood any better.

Despite its yellowing paper and frayed edges, the poster conserved an unignorable energy. More professional design and printing would have maximized the effect but dulled the edge of its indignation.

"How much?"

He overcharged me, but in the best traditions of the *brocante* I didn't haggle.

Meanwhile, the market for memorabilia of *les événements* remains healthy. Even for cobblestones. Recently an entrepreneur bought up a few hundred of them, cleaned them off, numbered them sequentially, and sold them as art objects. For €150, you could even have one gold-plated. As for the poster, restored and framed, it hangs in the front hall of our apartment. People tell me it's worth a lot more than I paid.

Revolution has not only its seasons but a price as well.

✳ ·38· ✳

SOMETHING FISHY

*Sydney Stadium. August 1968. A packed house for
the folk trio of Peter, Paul and Mary. As a change
from white-bread protest ("If I had a hammer"? Seriously?), Peter Yarrow introduces Boris Vian's "Le
Déserteur." "I'm sure I don't need to explain its message," he says. People look puzzled, even more so when
the trio begins the song in French. Barely a handful
understand the words, but perhaps that's the point.
With our troops fighting beside the United States in
Vietnam, it's a brave man who would proclaim in any
language, as Vian does, "And I will say to people /
Refuse to obey / Refuse to do it / Don't go to war."*

"ARE YOU GOING TO THE FESTIVAL OF SAINT JACQUES?" ASKED
our American friends the O'Days.

Praise be for visitors. Without them, we would never hear about
most seasonal events taking place outside our corner of Paris. The
arrondissements can be as intellectually isolated from one another as
villages were physically remote in medieval times.

"Who was Saint Jacques, anyway?" asked Bob O'Day. "Jacques—what's that in English? James?"

Another thing about visitors: They're inquisitive. They assume we're as interested in Paris as they are. In fact, we mostly take the city for granted. Maybe Sarah Bernhardt did live in this building, but to us it's where our dentist has his office.

"Yes, Jacques is the same as James," I said. "But I don't know what he has to do with seafood."

"Seafood?" They looked surprised.

"Saint Jacques is a kind of shellfish. You call them scallops. I guess this festival is some sort of promotion."

"Not religious, then?" They looked disappointed. All that expensive camera equipment, and no colorful folkloric rituals to record.

We agreed to accompany them anyway, and planned to meet the following Saturday afternoon on what turned out to be one of the windiest corners of Montmartre, just opposite the cemetery. Arriving ten minutes early, I took refuge in a café, a gesture as automatic to Parisians as sheltering under a tree.

Tourists enter cafés to drink coffee and scribble postcards that begin, "Writing this in the cutest café." To Parisians, they're an amenity: somewhere to get out of the rain, use the toilet, make a phone call, or kill time before a rendezvous. Any coffee one buys is rent. Historians of the Lost Generation will tell you that writers and artists hung out in cafés for the conversation. More likely it was because the toilets were clean.

When the O'Days and Marie-Dominique arrived, we walked with them down twisting rue Lepic. As we passed the Café des Deux Moulins, where Amélie Poulain worked in the famous film, the keening sound of bagpipes floated up the hill.

At the next corner, a crowd had gathered around six pipers and a drummer playing on the sidewalk. After the drone of Scottish pipes, the Breton variety can sound shrill, but these players were experts. So were the women in long blue dresses, arms over one another's shoulders, who danced in the street, their white lace bonnets nodding. Both pipers and dancers were well costumed, almost professionally so. I looked past them to a large open-front fish shop, where men were busy shoveling the orange fan-shaped shells of Saint Jacques into plastic bags. Business looked good. The presence of the pipers and dancers wasn't exactly coincidental.

Two men left the crowd to spontaneously link arms with the ladies and join their dance, if you could call it a dance: one step left, slide the other foot next to it, hop, and stamp, then repeat—slide . . . hop . . . stamp . . .

Something about the movement looked familiar. There was something of Greek dancing in it, but I'd seen Hopi and Navajo people dancing like this too, shuffling and stamping, deerskin moccasins raising the soft dust. Australian aboriginals too, in corroboree . . .

This was ur-dance, the irreducible minimum of calculated movement, the seed from which would germinate Pavlova, Balanchine, Nureyev—and Nijinsky's choreography for *Le Sacre du printemps*.

"You don't want to join in?" Bob joked.

With a little encouragement, he probably would have done so. That's another thing about visitors: they participate.

We continued down rue Lepic. It narrowed as café tables and chairs crowded onto the sidewalk, then it widened into Place des Abbesses.

Saint Denis, the patron saint of Paris, was decapitated by Roman soldiers at the foot of the hill. Legend says he rose to his feet and continued the climb toward Montmartre, carrying his head, which all the while continued to deliver a sermon about forgiveness.

He was supposed to have paused near this square and washed his face at a spring before pressing on for another five kilometers. It may be an index of Parisian skepticism about Denis and his headless perambulation that there's no church on the site. Only a modest subterranean chapel marks the spot.

Instead, the attractive little square shamelessly celebrates the bohemian lifestyle of Montmartre. Most weekends, the antique *manège* (carousel) keeps kids occupied snatching for the dangling tassel, the French equivalent of the brass ring. A green-painted Wallace water fountain with its four caryatids offers fresh water next to the art nouveau glass-and-iron metro entrance by Hector Guimard, rescued from the busier station at Hôtel de Ville and reerected here in 1974, out of harm's way.

Today, the carousel and fountain were inaccessible. Instead, white tents crowded every corner of the square. Men and women in aprons and caps shelled and shucked oysters, grilled skewers of

Saint Jacques, and ladled cups of soup. There was no room for dancing, even that shuffling step we'd seen earlier, but under an awning
six men with impressive beards were harmonizing, more or less, on
one of those folkish tunes beloved of pub bands around the world.

Couples bundled up against the cold strolled by, drinking from
flutes. Bob disappeared, to return with a bottle of champagne and
a handful of glasses. By then Deidre had also drifted away, but returned equally loaded down with a plate of mini–hamburger buns,
in each of which was sandwiched a slice of *jambon cru* and a whole
fat Saint Jacques.

As we juggled glasses and paper plates, a complete stranger
standing next to us, glass in hand, turned and announced in French,
"Isn't this wonderful? Wine, food, a beautiful day. Who could ask
for more?"

We raised our glasses in agreement. No place like Paris. No
place at all.

Since our conversation about the Republican calendar on the balcony overlooking the Canal Saint-Martin, I'd become more friendly
with Adrian de Grandpré, the historian priest.

I wish I'd encountered someone like him during my Catholic
boyhood instead of our beery Irish pastors, most of whom, we assumed, had been exiled to rural Australia in punishment for some
unmentionable transgression. His straightforward manner was the
best possible advertisement for his beliefs. The less he talked about
religion, the more interesting it became.

Author with musicians at the Saint Jacques festival.

He was also refreshingly unfussy when it came to Catholic dogma. Just the man to clarify the religious connections, if any, between Saint Jacques and the shellfish that bears his name.

It was typical of him that we met in a Starbucks in Montparnasse, where he had set up his laptop. This wasn't as incongruous as it sounds. France is the only country with a bishop of the internet. His name is Jacques Gaillot. When the church, because of his radical politics, fired him as bishop of Évreux, the pope placed him in charge of Parthenia, a defunct see in North Africa that expired in the fifth century. Gaillot announced mischievously that he regarded himself as a "virtual bishop," responsible for the moral well-being of that other incorporeal world, cyberspace.

"Is Saint Jacques the patron saint of Brittany?" I asked.

"Where did you see that?"

"Wikipedia."

Adrian sighed and shut his Mac. "Another reason not to trust the internet."

"So he isn't a patron? Or isn't a saint?"

"This 'patron saint' business is misleading. Saints aren't allocated to particular districts or trades. It's more that people with special interests select a saint as someone to pray to, since he or she might understand their specific difficulties."

"Like Denis and headaches?" Asking the decapitated Denis for relief from headache had always seemed to me one of the least likely opportunities for saintly intervention. "Or Saint Jude?" As the patron saint of lost causes, Jude is frequently invoked in the film business, a profession overendowed with desperation.

"Jude isn't a good example, actually," Adrian said. "He wrote in one of his letters that we should persevere in difficult circumstances. That's about it. I'm sure plenty of other saints said the same thing."

"Well, Saint Christopher, then?"

"Patron saint of travelers?" He shook his head. "There's some doubt that there even was such a person. The first reference appears in a thirteenth-century legend that reads like Harry Potter. He was dropped from the church calendar in 1969. That should tell you something."

"But Jacques—or rather James—really existed?"

"Oh, yes. There were two of them, actually. But neither went anywhere near Brittany. And neither was a fisherman."

"So how did he get to be the saint of a shellfish?"

"You'll laugh. Best theory? Boats carrying pilgrims from Britain on their way to the shrine of Saint James at Compostela in Spain would berth in Breton ports. Maybe some merchant put up a sign saying, 'Pilgrims of Saint Jacques Welcome Here.' You can see how it might happen."

I remembered the pipers and dancers outside the fish shop on rue Lepic. Yes, I could see very well.

✳ ·39· ✳

VIVE LE MISTRAL!

Vert-Galant, Paris 1ere. 12:30 a.m. 15°C. Dark as death, the Seine sucks at the ancient stones edging this tiny park. A willow trails fronds in the water, like a curtain sometimes obscuring and sometimes revealing the lights of the Louvre on the opposite bank. Rats scuttle by the water line, indifferent to both history and art. When all this has sunk back to the ooze, they will survive.

WHEN I FIRST VISITED PARIS IN THE 1970S, BUSKERS WERE OUT-numbered by mimes. On weekends, individually or in troupes, they congregated in particular on the sloping plaza in front of the Centre Pompidou, where crowds waiting to enter the exhibitions provided a captive audience.

Marcel Marceau and Bip, his chalk-faced alter ego with the squashed top hat surmounted by a flower, were at the peak of their fame, and some ambitious performers came to Paris to study with him, or with competitors such as Étienne Decroux. Among those doggedly climbing imaginary stairs and struggling to escape from glass cages was future Hollywood star Jessica Lange. She may even have participated in a group mime popular at the time, one I always remembered because of its association with the weather.

In this variation on the slow-motion walk, another mime standby, performers—sometimes singly, sometimes in pairs—battled an imaginary gale. Dressed uniformly in jumpsuits of metallized fabric, they struggled, head down and bent almost double, to advance in the face of a nonexistent hurricane, slogging a few painful steps only to be driven inexorably backward.

Hoping to refresh my memory, I combed the internet for a single image or film of this performance but found nothing. Nor have experts on mime ever heard of it. The phantom wind battled by these performers had swept the pavements clean, leaving no sign of their struggles.

Occasionally, such gaps in information intrigue the science-fiction writer in me. Perhaps they were not mimes at all but travelers from another time, briefly visible to us as they flickered in and out of this universe, only to slip back into an eternal gale howling in another. And why not? I never spoke to those people, nor did they communicate with their audience. Because to do so would offend against the mime's code? Or because they were not really of our world?

But anyone to whom I mentioned this speculation regarded me with amusement or incredulity, or both. (The surrealists would have understood. Where was André Breton when you needed him?)

I'd put the whole question of imaginary gales out of my mind until chance and the seasons reminded me.

In early January—on the twelfth night after Christmas, to be exact, and better known in the United States as the Epiphany—the French celebrate the Nuit des Rois, or Night of Kings, that day when the kings Gaspard, Melchior, and Balthazar arrived in Bethlehem with gifts for the baby Jesus of gold, frankincense, and myrrh (none of which, probably by intention, figures among the plants and minerals of the *Calendrier républicain*).

The French celebrate this festival by sharing a rich, buttery cake known as the *galette des rois*, or "kings' cake," made from layers of puff pastry filled with almond paste.

Like most things in France, the eating of the cake, customarily a family occasion, is accompanied by a ceremony. A gold paper crown is sold with each cake, and a tiny ceramic figure, or *fève*, about the size of a kidney bean is baked into every one.

Once the group is assembled, the galette is cut into as many slices as there are guests and glasses are filled with wine, traditionally champagne. The person who finds the *fève* in his or her portion (almost invariably the youngest) receives the crown, chooses someone at the table as prince or princess, and drops the *fève* into their glass. Wine is then poured over it, and to cries of "La reine [or Le roi] boit"—"the queen [or king] drinks"—everyone toasts their health.

After the last Nuit des Rois, Louise gave me a fève. "I got this in the galette at a party," she said. "It's more your kind of thing."

Usually *fèves* had a religious theme, but this one was decidedly secular: the tiny figure of a blond girl, her skirt blown high up her back, revealing a red thong. The plinth on which she stood was inscribed "Vive le Mistral!"

Certain winds are characteristic of the districts where they occur, mostly because of the damage they cause.

In Sydney the Southerly Buster, a cold squall, barrels out of the Indian Ocean at sunset to overturn yachts and drive the last sunbathers from the beach. In Switzerland the warm, dry wind called the Foehn rushes down the lee slopes of the Alps, inciting to irrational acts the normally staid citizens of such cities as Munich. And every resident of Los Angeles knows the atmospheric disturbances immortalized by Raymond Chandler: "those hot dry Santa Anas that come down through the mountain passes and curl your hair and make your nerves jump and your skin itch. Meek little wives feel the edge of the carving knife and study their husbands' necks."

Southern France has the Mistral. The people of Provence, who companionably call it "le mistraou," will tell you it doesn't deserve its bad reputation. But they are used to it. To the visitor, this river of air, steady and cold, flowing for days at a time down the valleys of the Rhône, across the swamps of the Camargue, over the Alpes-Maritimes and the coast to the Mediterranean, is a curse, abrading the nerves, destroying the environment, chilling their very souls.

"The Mistral *wants* you to defy it," said the poet André Verdet. When it blows, most often as the seasons change, nothing exists between the high blue sky with its smears of cirrus and the fields

Caricature of the Mistral, 1905.

cowering behind lines of cypresses and palisades of cane. Over millennia it has eroded the landscape, sandpapering the limestone peaks of the Alpilles into crags to which such towns as Les Baux cling like survivors from a medieval fable, inviting a sky filled with dragons.

Watching film of pedestrians battling the Mistral, heads down, hands clutching hats or holding down skirts, reminded me of those mime artists fighting a phantom wind on the slope before the Centre Pompidou. Maybe the person who choreographed their performance didn't come from anywhere as remote as another dimension—just from Arles or Saint-Rémy-de-Provence, where resistance to an implacable wind was part of the way of life.

Antique engraving of the Mistral.

40

ONE-MAN SHOW

Avignon, Vaucluse. July 1991. 11 p.m. 23°C. Late-night performance of Opéra équestre *by the Barta-bas theater group. Beneath indifferent stars, a woman's voice rises in alien vocalese. Stepping out of the shadows, she circles the sanded ring. Her red-and-gold costume marks her as Berber, an Arab of the Sahara. She cradles a shrouded bundle, the object of her lament. A dead child? Kneeling, she unwraps the swaddling and, sobbing, shows us . . . the head of a white horse.*

EVERY FOREIGN RESIDENT OF PARIS BECOMES AT SOME TIME A guide, whether they like it or not. The city and its customs are so intricate, its history so complex, that to leave the visitor to his or her own devices can appear cruel, even inhuman.

Even so, I resisted the role for more than a decade, and only surrendered when the literary event I helped run was in need of someone to lead a literary walk. Within a year, I was doing them two or three times a week during the warmer months—yet another

Parisian adjusting to the weather and the seasons, fulfilling a duty that came with the territory.

These walks were exhausting, not so much for the walking as for the performance that went with them. Untrained as an actor, I knew none of the techniques by which professionals conserved their energy. After three hours "onstage," I needed a couple of hours lying down in a dark room.

All of which made me more respectful of those performers who not only conducted audiences around a private world but also invented that world and the people who populated it.

I don't remember exactly when I met Hans Peter Litscher. He seems to have always been there, head and shoulders above the crowd at a party, deep in conversation with the most beautiful woman in the room. Tall, bespectacled, bearded, graying, in a ground-sweeping overcoat and with a thick scarf wrapped around his throat, he might have just stepped in from some high and chilly place. Even in summer, one would not be surprised to see him brush a snowflake from his shoulder or shake frost from his hair.

Hans Peter was born in Switzerland but is at home everywhere. His eccentric theater pieces are so uncategorizable that they have a category of their own, Litscheriade. For an opera company with too many sopranos on the payroll he conceived a libretto in which a wandering dwarf stumbles on a community of seven Snow Whites. A German town in need of tourists paid him to transform a decaying hotel into an upmarket chamber of horrors, supposedly the inn

Hans Peter Litscher and friend.

where Alfred Hitchcock spent his honeymoon and which inspired his career of shock and suspense.

In each case Hans Peter appeared as part of the show, a critic and musicologist explaining the background to the piece, a curator conducting visitors through a museum of memorabilia.

I learned not to be startled by his unannounced appearances at our door, a beribboned box in hand from the season's trendiest patisserie and with a fund of stories about his latest project.

"I don't suppose," he said during one such visit, "that you know where I can find a kangaroo costume?"

Remembering an Australian film that used one, I loaned him the DVD. A few months later we were invited to the premiere of *In Search of Eleonora Duse's Red-Headed Boxing Kangaroo* at the Swiss Cultural Center in Paris.

After the few dozen spectators assembled in what looked like a small regional museum, the curator—Hans Peter, of course—descended from upstairs, greeted us, and proceeded to explain, with reference to the exhibits in the glass cases, how Italian actress Eleonora Duse, star of the late-nineteenth-century stage, had rescued a boxing kangaroo from a circus and taken it with her on her travels, smuggling it into the most fashionable hotels of Europe. For the second half of the show we moved to a small theater, where we heard further tales of Duse and Marcel Proust and Duse's lover Gabriele D'Annunzio, spun by Hans Peter, now dressed as a kangaroo.

His fantasizing was seductive. A few days after seeing him in the Duse show, I found a battered single volume of one novel from Proust's *In Search of Lost Time*. The label of a lending library in Karachi showed it to have last been checked out in 1922. I sent it to Hans Peter with a long and rambling letter in a shaky hand, supposedly from a descendant of the man who caught and trained Duse's kangaroo and, through her, became a friend of Proust's. Next time the piece is staged, I fully expect to see both the book and letter included.

Two years ago, a press release for the latest Litscheriade arrived in the mail. His subject this time was close to my area of expertise.

With Garbo in the Grigioni Canton, with Hans Peter Litscher. Exhibition, guided tours & performances in Chur, Klosters, and Samedan.

What could have moved a breathtakingly beautiful Hollywood icon to put an abrupt end to her movie career at the age of thirty-seven, and thenceforth spend her summers at the far end of the Prättigau valley in Graubünden?

Staying in unassuming hotels at first and in a rented apartment later, Greta Garbo spent her days taking walks and practicing yoga until she passed away on April 15, 1990, at age eighty-five.

Hans Peter Litscher was intrigued precisely by the many blanks surrounding the mystery guest of Klosters. He embarked upon a quest to find the traces that Garbo left behind in Graubünden and to reassemble the mosaic of her life there, stone by stone. In Klosters, he found x-rays of Garbo's feet, the cane, shoes, and clothes she wore, and innumerable objects Garbo used there at the end of her life.

Foremost among these treasures is the discovery of the estate of local shoe salesman and foot fetishist Chasper Caflisch (1947–1990). Mesmerized by Garbo's body language, he followed the diva's every step during her long visits here, stalked her, and recorded her life in minutest detail.

Shortly before his suicide on the anniversary of her

death, Caflisch assembled a veritable Garbo mausoleum in his mobile home. This "Taj Mahal on wheels" serves as the core of Hans Peter Litscher's Garbo production.

"So now it's Garbo," I said next time we met.

"I thought you'd find that interesting." He bit into an éclair. "I'll let you know when we do it in France. You must come."

"But there weren't *really* x-rays of Garbo's feet, were there?"

"Of course." He looked offended. "Why not?"

"And this obsessive collector, Caflisch. He's another of your creations, isn't he? Like Duse's kangaroo?"

"You don't believe in the kangaroo? How sad. But of *course* it's true about Garbo. Everyone knows she spent time at Klosters."

"Well, yes, but . . ."

"And it's common knowledge that she liked to walk."

"I suppose . . ."

"So why so skeptical? Incidentally, did I tell you the town council is thinking of renaming her favorite hill Piz Garbo, Mount Garbo?" He leaned forward. "Is there any more tea in the pot?"

As I poured, I said, "A pity this Caflisch isn't around to back up the story."

"But there's his documentation. You should see it. Maps, doctor's reports . . . He made a film about her. And composed some music—a serenade for wind instruments—dedicated to her."

"The score for which has since been lost, no doubt."

He shook his head sadly at such cynicism. "I see you will not let

Garbo and her feet.

yourself be convinced." He sighed. "Well, this has been most pleasant. Do you mind if I eat this last éclair?"

A few days later an anonymous email arrived, with a link to a posting on YouTube. *Greta Garbo at the Foot of the Magic Mountain.*

The film showed the stage in a small theater. Three musicians, a woman and two men, dressed in ethnic costumes, blew a lugubrious serenade on two-meter-long wooden alpenhorns, the native instrument of Switzerland. On the screen behind them, clips played from Garbo's movies, all of them featuring her feet: in ballet slippers for *Grand Hotel*, long leather boots for *Queen Christina*, clumpy brogues for *Anna Christie*.

Caught again, dammit!

41

EATING IN

The Benedictine abbey of Saint Peter, Hautvillers,
Marne. About 1670. Dom Pérignon, the cellarist in
charge of making wine from the grapes of the abbey's
vineyards, has been experimenting with a method of
producing the naturally sparkling wine that will one
day be known as Champagne. According to legend,
he announces his breakthrough by calling to his fellow
monks, "I am drinking stars!"

IT WAS YEARS SINCE I'D SPENT ANY TIME IN THE UNITED STATES,
long enough to think of Manhattan as a foreign country. Mentally
converting dollars to Euros became second nature, and the automatic "Have a nice day" of checkout ladies had me responding, to
their confusion, "Thanks. You too."

Some friends had lent me their apartment in Midtown. There's
a special satisfaction in the anonymity of a hotel room or someone
else's home, that sense of a neutral space that you are free to fill with
whatever you please. For the period of your sequestration, you are
whoever you choose to be. Leonard Cohen wrote about "laying low,

and letting the hunt go by." Something of that sense was the first pleasure of being back in New York.

"We've filled the fridge," said my friends as they left. "No need to buy anything."

But they were vegetarians (and I was anything but). The grains, greens, and soy products they'd left me were free of salt, preservatives, and, sadly, flavor.

Fortunately one is never more than a few blocks from one of those vast supermarkets that seem to occupy every second corner in American cities. Within thirty minutes I was standing just inside the entrance to such an establishment, speechless with admiration.

European markets have aisles; this one had avenues . . . boulevards . . . *freeways* of food. Fifty kinds of bread. Twenty kinds of muffins. Ten kinds of butter. Thirty varieties of milk. And the meats! Not just pork and beef but also buffalo and ostrich.

The produce department provided the greatest surprise. Dragon fruit, guavas, and rambutan were almost unknown in France, as were black potatoes, prickly pear, and tomatillos, but even more surprising were the familiar plants and fruits jumbled together with no respect for the seasons.

How could ears of sweet corn, traditionally available for only a few weeks in summer, be on sale next to forest mushrooms that grow only in the fall? Since this was high summer, one expected lettuces, but not white asparagus. And why were beige autumnal pears offered next to fat summery strawberries?

No merchant in Paris would offer this miscellany of produce at the same time of year. Timing was everything. Sicilian clementines arriving in December, each bearing a few green leaves, brought a tart, bright reminder of summer to the darkest of months and added a grace note to the rituals of Christmas. Passe-Crassanes, the juiciest of pears, identified by the blob of red wax on the end of each stem, were in season only for the same few weeks as unctuous Vacherin cheese, the taste of which they so perfectly complemented.

French markets used refrigeration too, but less promiscuously. Just because something could be done didn't mean it *should* be done. Melons could be had in December, flown in from Israel or Africa, but the connoisseur saved that experience for the summer, since nothing compared to the taste of a juicy cantaloupe from Cavaillon eaten with paper-thin slices of *jambon cru*, wind-dried all winter under the rafters of a Provençal farmhouse.

Moreover, to eat summer fruit in the depth of winter was to miss the pleasure of desserts unique to the colder months—a tarte Tatin of caramelized apples, or pears *à la Dijonnaise*, simmered in spiced and sugared white wine.

Loading up my supermarket cart with some more obscure products of its shelves, I hauled my purchases back to the apartment.

I'd just closed the refrigerator when jet lag struck, and I fell into bed. As it was only about 8 p.m. local time, I woke, refreshed, at 3 a.m. Fighting one's circadian rhythms is futile, so I brewed a pot of Outer Mongolian coffee, toasted a Transylvanian whole-grain muffin with Circassian date flakes, and settled down in front of the TV. After a few minutes staring in disbelief at evangelists promoting prayer handkerchiefs and cancer cures made from sacred buffalo tallow and consecrated water from the Jordan River, I took refuge in the all-movie channels.

We all enjoy doing something we know is not good for us, but it's an additional pleasure to have no choice. Watching *Down Argentine Way* with Betty Grable, Don Ameche, and Carmen Miranda in that vivid 1940s Technicolor gave the same guilty satisfaction as eating peaches out of the can, and not caring that the syrup dripped off your chin.

Browsing the produce aisles of that supermarket had brought home to me how much I'd learned from living in France. It taught me that, in food as in most things, the essence of pleasure resides in timing. To delay satisfaction sharpens the experience. Anticipation stimulates the imagination, enriching both the expectation of gratification and the gratification itself.

To eat summer fruit in midwinter felt as sinful as watching movies at 3 a.m. Much as I admired the miracle of hydroponics that brought strawberries to unnatural ripeness out of season, I wasn't tempted to try them. Somewhere in Charente or Languedoc, tiny *fraises des bois* were making their slow way to maturity. Soon they would arrive at the outdoor produce market on rue de Seine. I remembered their scent, almost like perfume, the subtle mixture of tart and sweet, the delicious crunch between tongue and palate.

I could wait.

42

A MAN MADE OF FLOWERS

Cabris, Alpes-Maritimes. October 2014. 9 p.m. 18°C.
A plaza paved in fieldstone ends abruptly at a cliff
that plunges hundreds of meters to the verdant coastal
strip, a patchwork of orchards and vineyards, veiled in
woodsmoke as farmers burn off the debris of the har-
vest. Beyond, the Mediterranean is a seductive ceru-
lean blue, deep enough to die in. In July 1944, Antoine
de Saint-Exupéry plunged his P-38 Lightning into its
embrace, his death, like his life, the embodiment of
a belief that "perfection is achieved not when there is
nothing more to add, but when there is nothing left to
take away."

FRANÇOIS MITTERRAND WASN'T THE ONLY POLITICIAN TO LINK HIS
career to the abundance of France's fields and orchards.

A contrast to the sly, suave, devious Mitterrand, the burly six-
foot-two-inch-tall Jacques Chirac, president from 1995 to 2007 following terms as prime minister and as mayor of Paris, was known

as "the Bulldozer." The name was conferred by his former boss, President Georges Pompidou, in recognition of his ability to get things done, never mind whom he crushed in the process.

In a distant echo of the *Calendrier républicain*, both Mitterrand and Chirac chose a fruit or flower as emblem of their time in office. It says something about their fundamental difference in style that Mitterrand selected the patrician rose, whereas Chirac opted for the more egalitarian apple.

Chirac's enthusiasm for apples became public while he was still mayor of Paris. After he mentioned they were his favorite fruit, a journalist confronted him with some samples of different types and asked if he could identify them. A variation on the old trick of discrediting a self-styled Man of the People by asking him the price of a liter of milk, the device was too crude for the savvy Chirac, who blasted the man by affirming his relish for all apples, irrespective of variety, providing only that they were French.

Of these there was no shortage. In defiance of the EU's attempt to position the bland Golden Delicious as a one-size-fits-all "Euroapple," French growers produced scores of varieties, from the hard, green Granny Smith to the wan and spotty Clochard, the yellow Chanticleer to the superjuicy Pink Lady, the red-brown Reinette to the tart Cox's Orange Pippin, and dozens in between. Each excelled in its own way. Clochards, despite their unprepossessing appearance, were ideal for baking with meat. Norman farmers favored bittersweet apples like the Binet Rouge for making cider. Against such competition, the Golden Delicious scored poorly. It appealed

Jacques Chirac and apples, 1991.

mostly to shippers, since the vaguely hexagonal shape made it easier to pack.

Chirac's enthusiasm for apples played so well that he made it the motif of his political career. In 1991, he replaced his mayoral chain of office with an improvised necklace of apples to greet a deputation of farmers. When he ran for president in 1995, his campaign logo was a green tree with bright red apples. This delighted journalists, who described him as "sitting pretty beneath his apple tree," "tending his orchard," and "harvesting the fruit of his labors." When the former president and onetime critic made conciliatory noises about Chirac, someone commented, "Giscard is eating apples."

Food became a theme of the election. A restaurant patronized by both Chirac and his opponent, Édouard Balladur, listed the favorite meals of both and invited other clients to participate in an informal poll by ordering one of the two dishes. Many more preferred Chirac's hearty country sausage than Balladur's prissy herrings in oil, a result reflected in Chirac's landslide victory.

In Shakespeare's *Macbeth*, a man is praised for having confessed his sins before being hanged. "Nothing in his life became him like the leaving it," says the man who officiated at his execution. The line can sound respectful but works better if played with black humor, like Greta Garbo's comment as the commissar in the film *Ninotchka* that "the last mass trials have been a great success. There are going to be fewer but better Russians."

Nothing became Mitterrand's life like the leaving it. In his fourteen years as president, he gained a reputation as someone who liked to eat. His private chef, Danièle Mazet-Delpeuch, the first woman to cook for a serving president, revealed that when he visited the kitchen at night in search of a snack, she made him the most luxurious of nibbles: toasted Poilâne wholemeal sourdough bread topped with thick slices of Périgord truffle at $3,000 a kilo.

When he could no longer disguise the progress of his final illness, the president chose to go out eating. On New Year's Eve 1995 he invited thirty friends to his holiday home at Latche, in the southwestern region of Landes, part of ancient Gascony, for a dinner of oysters; foie gras; capons, those fattest of all chickens; and, as a starter, ortolans.

A famous delicacy, these tiny birds, no bigger than a man's thumb, are trapped in mist nets, drowned in Armagnac, roasted in individual closed ceramic pots, and then eaten whole—bones, beak, and all. As each pot is opened, the diner drapes a napkin over his head—to conserve the aroma, but also, it's said, to hide his sinful act from God.

"Bien sûr, m'sieur le Président," said his chef after Mitterrand made his request. "However, I would be remiss in my duty if I did not point out that the ortolan is a protected species."

"I am president of the Republic," Mitterrand said wearily, "and have only a few weeks to live. What can they do to me?"

Accordingly, each diner, including the president, was served two ortolans. Eight days later he was dead, having ended his life as he lived it: on a full stomach.

✳ · 43 · ✳

POETS

Atelier Christian Dior, avenue Montaigne, Paris. February 12, 1947. Expecting a tentative collection reflecting postwar austerity, fashionistas are astonished by dresses containing, according to one report, "between fifteen and twenty-five yards of material, with tiny sashed waists in black broadcloth, tussore, and silk taffeta, each with a built-in corset that was itself a deeply disturbing work of art." In a reminder of couture's roots in nature and seasonality, Dior calls it "La Ligne corolle" (the Flower Line), but Carmel Snow, editor of Harper's Bazaar, *prefers "the New Look."*

WHILE BUSINESSMEN, BUREAUCRATS, PRIESTS, AND FARMERS breathed a collective sigh of relief at the demise of the Republican calendar, some poets, musicians, and artists regretted the return of the Gregorian model.

Many sympathized with Fabre's attempt, however clumsy, to reimagine nature as a kind of poem. British novelist Thomas Hardy, who celebrated rural life in such novels as *Far from the Madding*

Crowd and *Tess of the d'Urbervilles*, spoke for many when he wrote, "I feel that Nature is played out as a Beauty, but not as a Mystery. I don't want to see landscapes. . . . I want to see the deeper reality underlying the scenic, the expression of what are sometimes called abstract imaginings."

Lafitte's paintings for the calendar revived his career, relaunching him as a decorator and designer. Widely circulated and massively reproduced, the paintings became the calendar's standard illustrations and most enduring monument.

His image for Messidor, the month of the grain harvest, may have inspired one of the greatest of all poets. Lafitte represents the harvest as a woman asleep against a sheaf of wheat, sickle by her side. Red flowers droop at the edges of the picture and lie on her lap, and the verse refers to "the day's labor succeeded by a sweet sleep."

Twenty years later John Keats, in "To Autumn," would also compare the season to an exhausted harvester and employ almost identical imagery:

> *Who hath not seen thee oft amid thy store?*
> *Sometimes whoever seeks abroad may find*
> *Thee sitting careless on a granary floor,*
> *Thy hair soft-lifted by the winnowing wind;*
> *Or on a half-reap'd furrow sound asleep,*
> *Drows'd with the fume of poppies, while thy hook*
> *Spares the next swath and all its twined flowers . . .*

Messidor *by Louis Lafitte*.

Poets, particularly those of the decadent movement that flourished in France during the last quarter of the nineteenth century, embraced the idea that nature could embody human emotions. Paul Verlaine's "Chanson d'automne" ("Autumn Song") became one of the most popular of all French poems:

> *The long sobs of autumn's violins*
> *Wound my heart with a monotonous languor.*
> *Suffocating and pallid, when the clock strikes,*
> *I remember the days long past and I weep.*
> *And I set off in the rough wind that carries me*
> *Hither and thither like a dead leaf.*

He was equally moved by moonlight. In *Clair de Lune*, he wrote:

> *The calm, pale moonlight, whose sad beauty, beaming,*
> *Sets the birds softly dreaming in the trees,*
> *And makes the marbled fountains, gushing, streaming—*
> *Slender jet-fountains—sob their ecstasies.*

Fiction too found this new technique useful. Traditionally, novels relied on conversations, letters, or authorial musings to carry a story. Descriptions of landscape or weather were rare. During the last half of the nineteenth century, however, novelists began using nature to amplify a character or establish a mood, sometimes specifically evoking the Republican calendar. For his 1885 novel about a strike among coal miners in northern France, Émile Zola chose the title *Germinal*. It concluded, "Men were springing forth, a black avenging army, germinating slowly in the furrows, growing towards the harvests of the next century, and their germination would soon overturn the earth."

Filmmakers would seize on the symbolism of nature to augment often feeble stories and third-rate performers. Storms conveyed passion, flowers romance. Higher aspirations were suggested by sunrises and sunsets, or by the camera staring meaningfully at the sky. Images of flowers, insects, and nesting birds to illustrate procreation passed so quickly into the language that "the birds and the bees" became shorthand for sex education.

To songwriters, the language of Fabre and Lafitte was likewise a gift. Jacques Prévert's lyrics for one of the most popular of French chansons, Joseph Kosma's "Les Feuilles mortes" (dead leaves), compares sad memories to leaves carried away by "the wind of forgetting." Charles Trenet, writing of the sea in "La Mer," suggests that the "love song" of the sea has "cradled my heart."

Both songs became even more successful in English versions, though in each case the new lyrics coarsened the message. Eva Cassidy's reworking of Prévert's song as "Autumn Leaves" compared dead leaves, obscurely, to "your lips, the summer kisses / The sunburned hands I used to hold." In his version of "La Mer," Bobby Darin turned Trenet's paean to the waves and his clouds like sheep guarded by angelic shepherdesses into the finger-snapping "Beyond the Sea," in which "somewhere, waiting for me, a lover stands on golden sands."

Having a new means of speaking of the seasons continues to tempt poets and lyricists. In the sixties, songwriter Hugues Aufray made the months of the Republican calendar into a love story:

> *White is the snow in Nivôse,*
> *Gray is the rain in Pluviôse.*
> *Black is the wind in Ventôse.*
> *We met one another in Germinal,*
> *We fell in love in Floréal*
> *And got married in Prairial.*
> *The child was born in Messidor,*
> *He grew up in Thermidor*
> *And then left in Fructidor.*
> *Life is white in Vendémiaire,*
> *Life is gray in Brumaire,*
> *And then life is black in Frimaire.*

Using nature to mirror human feelings doesn't appeal to everyone, least of all plain-speaking Anglo-Saxons. In 1856, art theorist John Ruskin coined the term "pathetic fallacy" to describe the belief that autumn might "sob" or birds "softly dream." In his view, "Objects . . . derive their influence not from properties inherent in them . . . but from such as are bestowed upon them by the minds of those who are conversant with or affected by these objects." As for weather, it was, he insisted, just weather: "Sunshine is delicious, rain is refreshing, wind braces us up, snow is exhilarating; there is really no such thing as bad weather, only different kinds of good weather."

The element of "Bah! Humbug!" in such comments found no sympathy across the Channel. Both Freud and Jung conceded that elements of the natural world can affect us deeply. How ironic if one of the most enduring legacies of the revolution should be not that of either Danton or Robespierre but of the fraudulent and swindling Fabre d'Églantine.

❊ ·44· ❊

NIGHT CREATURES

Reid Hall, Paris 6me. November 2017. 6°C. Hol-
lins University of Roanoke, Virginia, has invited
some distinguished expatriates to speak at a lunch for
a group of visiting alumni. During a discussion on-
stage between Terrance Gelenter and Diane Johnson,
a member of the audience asks, "What do you miss
most about the United States?" Both reply in unison,
"Mexican food."

"IT'S SAD," SAID TERRANCE GELENTER.

Across the table at the Chez Fernand, his bearded face, never notably cheerful, did look more than usually doleful.

"Cheer up," I said. "If it makes you feel any better, I'll pick up the check."

Normally this was enough to lighten his mood, but not today.

"I didn't mean *I* was sad," he said. "Though I am. I meant SAD. Seasonal Affective Disorder. It always affects me at this time of year. Paris starts to get me down."

"Really?"

SAD results in part from a lack of sunshine. I looked out at narrow, restaurant-lined rue Guisarde. Like most such streets in Saint-Germain, it only sees direct sunlight around midday, but the locals didn't seem to mind. Living in perpetual shadow encourages a collective good humor, a sense of us-against-them that has seen them through tough times, much as the "Britain Can Take It" spirit sustained London through the Blitz.

But Gelenter was from suburban New York, so allowances had to be made. As Thomas Wolfe suggested in one of his novels, only the dead know Brooklyn. A certain melancholy was to be expected.

"What form does it take, this SAD?"

"Oh, you know, anxiety, depression, sleeplessness . . . It's a recognized condition. Say, do you think the girl heard you order the wine?"

Just then, he looked past my shoulder and his eyes lit up. I guessed the waitress was heading in our direction.

"Ah, *ma jolie* . . ." Half rising, he reached out his hand. I thought for a moment he might clamber over the table, and me as well, in his haste to get to her. Abruptly he had become the boulevardier *par excellence*.

This was a performance polished to a gleam by repetition. He probably didn't realize any longer that he was doing it. Seeing an attractive woman between the ages of fifteen and ninety— policewoman, nun, mother of eight: it didn't matter—he was energized as if a switch had been thrown, and suddenly there was Terrance le Coquin (Naughty Terrance).

Terrance Gelenter in repose.

What would he do if one of these women said "OK" and hitched up her skirt? I suspected he would run a mile, but so far I'd never been around when this happened, if it ever did.

To distract him, I took the *pichet* of Bordeaux and poured each of us a glass. For a moment he wavered, his barrage of double entendres challenged by the appeal of a drink. Eventually the bird (or rather, glass) in the hand won over the bird who remained beyond his grasp.

"Salut," he said, settling back into his chair and taking a swallow.

"Salut," I said. "So . . . you can't sleep?"

"Yeah. It's a *bêtise*. The other night, it was so bad I got out of bed and went for a walk."

"What sort of time was this?"

"I don't know . . . two or three."

"You went walking at two or three a.m. because you were depressed?"

"Sure. Why not?" He emptied his glass and reached for the *pichet*. "And to see who I could pick up, of course." He opened the menu. "How's the *boeuf bourguignon* here?"

Walking the streets at 3 a.m. wasn't as novel for me as I suggested. All my life I've worked best after dark, rising regularly at 4 a.m., brain humming with ideas. People like me relish the night's peace and tranquility, its quality of repose. The English term "night owl" belittles us. Unlike that cruising predator of the woods and fields, we spend our nights in reflection, reading, writing, and, to facilitate the process, occasionally roaming empty streets. Acknowledging our affinity with the world of dream, the French call us *noctambules* (nightwalkers).

Woody Allen is the latest recruit to our group. In his film *Midnight in Paris*, a restless American screenwriter played by Owen Wilson gets lost during a late-night stroll and is picked up by a vintage car that carries him back to the Paris of Hemingway and Fitzgerald and Kiki of Montparnasse.

The film is charming enough, but others have done it better: Philippe Soupault's *Last Nights of Paris*, Louis Aragon's *Paris Peasant*, or Henry Miller's *Quiet Days in Clichy* with photographs by another insomniac, Gyula Halász, alias Brassaï.

The list of *noctambules* goes back to Henri de Toulouse-Lautrec, who found little to draw in Paris by day but ample material in the gloom and glare of Montmartre's nights—which also hid his physical deformities. He didn't lack company. Prostitutes and their clients came out as the sun went down. So did the men who pasted his posters to Montmartre's walls—followed closely by collectors, who peeled his vivid paper masterpieces off the brickwork before the glue had time to set.

Paris is no twenty-four-hour city like Hong Kong, Tokyo, or Los Angeles. You will look in vain for an all-night supermarket, cinema, or restaurant. The average Parisian returns home at night, eats dinner, watches TV, and goes to bed. That some people are of the day and others of the night is acknowledged, but not catered to. We *noctambules* must make our own arrangements.

As a matter of form, the city administration discourages us.

Sunset sees public parks locked. Restaurants close around midnight, cafés at 2 a.m.; cooks and waiters have home lives too. The Métro ceases around 1 a.m. Yet as one door closes, another is left slightly ajar. Intermittent Noctambuses (night buses) serve the sleepless, and a few cafés stay open all night, ostensibly for the benefit of newspapermen and others who work unsocial hours but in fact havens for the restless and, in the words of one habitué, "people who want to be alone but need company for it." In the most famous of these twenty-four-hour cafés, Montparnasse's Le Sélect, James Baldwin wrote most of his first novel, *Giovanni's Room*, and Hart Crane, gifted poet of "The Bridge," drank away his nights, brawling with waiters over the bill and more than once ending up in jail.

Though I was only twelve when I first read Dylan Thomas's poem "In My Craft or Sullen Art," I recognized instantly a desire shared with him to "in the still night / When only the moon rages . . . labour by singing light." The dark was always my home. In a country of blazing sun, I gravitated perversely toward the lightless space of *Astounding Science Fiction* magazine, the ruined Vienna of Graham Greene's *The Third Man*, and Raymond Chandler's Los Angeles, where "the streets were dark with something more than night." Murmuring at my ear as I read was a shortwave radio broadcasting Voice of America's nightly program of modern jazz, a thread of sound connecting me to Minton's and Birdland and the Lighthouse at Hermosa Beach. I was home.

Jazz, that ultimate music of the night, is the Esperanto of the *noctambule*. One winter night not long after I moved to France, I

heard an a cappella vocal trio called Les Amuse-Gueules perform in
a bleak municipal hall by the Canal Saint-Martin. Their repertoire
included Thelonious Monk's bebop classic "Well You Needn't."

> You're talkin' so sweet well you needn't
> You say you won't cheat well you needn't
> You're tappin' your feet well you needn't
> It's over now, it's over now.

I felt like a traveler in a remote corner of the world who hears
someone speak his own language. How often, talking to some
French writer or artist of my generation, I'd seen their eyes light
up at the mention of a favorite track. "'A Night in Tunisia'? Yes,
of course I know it. Which version do you prefer, Monk's or Dizzy
Gillespie's?" Until then, it had never crossed my mind that people
in France heard those same Voice of America broadcasts, that exis-
tentialism evolved to the music of Monk, Miles Davis, and Charlie
"Bird" Parker.

Jazz gave me something in common with Albert Camus, Jean-
Paul Sartre, Simone de Beauvoir, Boris Vian, and Juliette Gréco. It
ignored intellectual disciplines. In 1949, Charlie Parker chatted with
Jean-Paul Sartre at the Club Saint-Germain. "I'm very glad to have
met you," he told Sartre as they parted. "I like your playing very
much." A writer may improvise just as powerfully with words and
ideas as a musician can with an instrument.

Modern jazz is an art of the night. So is sex. "Night, beautiful courtesan," mused Apollinaire. In "Paris at Night," Jacques Prévert wrote:

> *Three matches, one by one struck in the night*
> *The first to see your face in its entirety*
> *The second to see your eyes*
> *The last to see your mouth*
> *And the darkness to remind me of all these*
> *As I squeeze you in my arms.*

"I couldn't believe what I was hearing," murmured my actress friend Anna. She was describing some neighbors she'd met just a few doors down the street in the early hours of the morning.

We were sitting in a café on rue François Miron, a narrow thoroughfare that snaked along the edge of the Marais, the most medieval of the inner districts. Its churches and *hôtels particuliers* had already been old and leaning when François Villon reeled among them, shouting, "We must know who we are. Get to know the monster that lives in your soul; dive deep and explore it."

I thought I knew who these people were, but the following Sunday around midnight, stepping out onto the narrow sidewalk in front of her building, I turned right and walked toward the knot of people standing outside No. 14. A light rain sifted down through the streetlights, adding a sheen to the ancient stones.

The seventeenth-century exterior of No. 14 looked unremarkable. Exposed beams and crooked windows gave no hint that it housed one of Paris's most popular sex clubs. On the first of its three floors, clients could enjoy a buffet supper, dance in the disco, and drink at the bar—and then they could descend to the lower levels to test the limits of what was possible between consenting adults.

Ironically, one of the few forbidden acts was smoking. To light up, patrons had to ascend to the street. About a dozen, mostly women, huddled against the façade to escape the rain. Most wore long coats, a few of them fur, but I spotted a Burberry, and one woman was tightly wrapped, Marlene Dietrich–like, in a belted garment of black leather that brought to mind horse whips and handcuffs. All wore heels so high that to walk more than a block invited a broken ankle. Not that any of them needed to walk. For each, a chauffeur or obliging husband dozed in a nearby side street or parking lot, half listening to late-night radio, awaiting their summons.

As I passed, a few of the women turned away and lowered their voices, but most continued to murmur into their cell phones. I caught snatches of conversation in German, English, French. ". . . thought I was going to faint . . . *son bite . . . enorme, ma biche, je te jure . . .*"

Anna had been incredulous when I explained about *échangiste* clubs. I found them all too easy to understand. These were the people for whom Dylan Thomas had written:

> . . . *the lovers, their arms*
> *Round the griefs of the ages,*

Who pay no praise or wages
Nor heed my craft or art.

He would have rejoiced in the existence of these fellow *noctam-bules*, as would Prévert and Aragon and Villon. As did I. Respect must be shown.

"How about another bottle?" I said to Naughty Terrance.

45

THE WEATHER AT WAR

Mérignac Airfield, near Bordeaux. June 17, 1940.
8 a.m. 15°C. A small plane sent by Winston Churchill
takes off. Among its passengers is Charles de Gaulle,
a junior general in the defeated army. Although France
has surrendered, he will defy orders and set up a Free
French government in London. He looks down on shat-
tered tanks lining the roads and a torpedoed ship, sink-
ing, with two thousand British troops on board. Years
later, André Malraux will ask what it was like. Grasp-
ing his hands, the general, deeply affected, says, "Oh,
Malraux. It was appalling."

THE GERMANS HAD FABULOUS WEATHER FOR THEIR INVASION.
Hitler's armies attacked Holland and Belgium on May 10. By June 14,
five weeks later, they had overrun those countries and were in Paris.
It didn't rain once. The Wehrmacht marched down the Champs-
Élysées under blue skies, perfect for the newsreel cameramen who
framed them with a background of the Arc de Triomphe.

Some say those sunny days lost Germany the war. Instead of

ordering an immediate amphibious assault on southern England that might have forced Britain to surrender, Hitler took time out to enjoy France. The official newsreel *Die Deutsche Wochenschau* filmed him on the esplanade of the Palais de Chaillot, overlooking the Champ de Mars and the Eiffel Tower, grinning as widely as any tourist.

How obliging of the French, he must have thought, to surrender so quickly, making it unnecessary to level Paris as he had Warsaw the previous fall. Now the city could serve as a rest-and-recreation center for the Reich. Every serviceman was promised at least one week's leave in Paris. Luftwaffe Oberleutnant Dietrich Schultz-Köhn, a familiar figure on the prewar Paris jazz scene, acted as emissary to the café and club owners, arranging entertainment for the troops. His efforts earned him the nickname "Doktor Jazz."

With the armistice of June 22, hostilities ceased. The armed forces stood down. A puppet government under the eighty-year-old World War I hero Marshal Philippe Pétain administered most of the country from the spa town of Vichy. The coasts and Paris remained under military rule.

Along the Atlantic, battalions of prisoners built submarine pens. Protected by 3.5 meters of solid concrete, the bases at Saint-Nazaire, Lorient, La Rochelle, and Bordeaux would survive the worst that Allied bombers could drop on them.

I know this area well. Once a year, as reliably as any migrating bird or upstream-swimming salmon, we close our Paris apartment, arrange for the concierge to water the plants and feed the cat, and retreat for two weeks to the southwest and the breezier, fresher, less complicated countryside of Charente, where Marie-Dominique's grandparents were thoughtful enough to bequeath her their spacious home in the village of Fouras.

Paris has few memorials to the occupation. Here and there, discreet marble tablets embedded in walls signify that some resistant died on this corner *pour la Patrie*. On anniversaries, a military charity attaches a bouquet to each memorial, using the metal ring conveniently provided. Otherwise, there are few tangible souvenirs. It's not something of which the French wish to be reminded. As the British novelist Sebastian Faulks wrote, "De Gaulle offered his battered country a fairy tale; we resisted the Germans and we freed ourselves by force of arms. His weary, disillusioned people were happy to accept this politically necessary fable."

Paradoxically, the occupation has left more signs in the country, particularly in areas like Charente, where the Nazis had time to put down roots. Incongruity makes such survivals stand out. A crumbling pillbox is more sinister for being surrounded by grazing cows, and a rusting metal pylon for the family of storks that has set up house on top. At the La Pallice submarine base a few kilometers outside La Rochelle, pleasure boats idle by as their owners peer into the dark from which wolf packs of U-boats once slipped out into the Atlantic. Today, the bases are maintained as locations for foreign filmmakers. Those at La Pallice were used in *Raiders of the Lost Ark* and *Das Boot*.

La Rochelle bears numerous signs of occupation. With twenty-two thousand Germans billeted in a town of only thirty-five thousand

Nazi bunker in La Rochelle.

people, its cafés, theaters, and cinemas were so completely engulfed that the Germans created their own.

The strangest began life as the best hotel in town, a four-story building down a quiet side street. As was typical, the officers of the Kriegsmarine moved in, which created a tempting target for local resistants or a precision bombing raid. The officers needed something solid to protect them from bombs; a shield as thick, in fact, as that protecting the submarine pens. With Teutonic thoroughness, engineers cleared the lowest floors of the hotel and filled the rooms with concrete.

Once the bombing intensified, the basement was enlarged to accommodate a small hospital. As they spent more time there, officers demanded a bar and a space for dancing. They decorated the walls with examples of Navy humor, and a few mermaids. An air-raid shelter became the town's hottest, indeed only, nightclub.

My guide to the bunker proudly informed me that his father, who had projected films for the Germans, also found the music they most enjoyed, scouring the city and surrounding districts for records by American big bands, in particular Count Basie, Duke Ellington, and Jimmie Lunceford. As Hitler frowned on such "decadent" music, one had to be cautious about discussing titles in the hearing of the more committed servants of the Reich. "Saint Louis Blues" became "La Tristesse de Saint Louis": "the sadness of Saint Louis."

As the war turned against Hitler, the garrisons in La Rochelle and the nearby town of Royan were trapped in a "pocket" with their backs to the sea. The Luftwaffe air-dropped supplies and other necessities, including movies. The last production of Studio Babelsberg before Berlin fell to the Russians was the historical epic *Kolberg*. Goering ordered a copy parachuted into the pocket, allowing a defiant joint Berlin–La Rochelle premiere to take place on January 30, 1945. Since the film dealt with a German city's resistance to Napoléon in 1806, when the whole population marched out against the enemy, the message was clear: La Rochelle was expected to hold out till the end.

Once I showed curiosity about the local history of the war years, word got around. Like shy animals nervous of the daylight, amateur conservators and armchair historians emerged from the shadows to show off their treasures.

"This will interest you," one bookseller said, taking what looked like a school exercise book from his locked cabinet. "It's a recipe book from 1943."

I leafed through the neatly handwritten pages. Eggs, cream, ham; soufflés, roast goose, even lobster thermidor.

"They lived well," I said. "I had no idea."

"Oh, I don't think the owner ever cooked these dishes. Everything was rationed. The Germans got anything good."

"Why compile this book, then?"

He shrugged. "Perhaps . . . to remember?" He replaced it reverently. "Think of it as . . . culinary pornography."

Fouras itself is too small to support a bookshop, but an enterprising bibliophile runs a stall in the market square. He hailed me one morning as I walked back from the *halles*, loaded with produce for lunch.

"I was talking to a friend in La Rochelle," he said. From under his table, he produced a carefully wrapped book. "Is this the kind of thing you're looking for?"

I put down the bags of cheese, peaches, and pâté. The family wouldn't mind waiting for lunch. And if they did . . . well, even in France, history could trump appetite.

The book, in a flimsy brown paper wrapper, was called *Occupation (1940–1945): Siège de La Rochelle*. I'd never heard of the writer,

Albert Miaux, but the fact that the book was published by an obscure press in La Rochelle suggested he wasn't a household name. (In fact, he wrote only one book, and I was holding it. Nor was it ever circulated more widely than the La Rochelle area.)

The text was made up of poems, illustrated with smudgy drawings. From a quick glance, Miaux was no Verlaine. What made the book interesting was his subject matter: He had created a poetic history of the occupation. There were poems about the exodus from La Rochelle as the Germans approached, people clogging the roads, possessions heaped on top of ancient automobiles; the triumphant troops in gray; the huddle of people under the colonnade outside the Kommandatura as the Germans imposed their restrictions on Jews and other non-Aryans. Here were glimpses of a submarine heading back to base at La Pallice and German officers dining on the products of the black market or enjoying a film with a mostly French audience, but also the roundup of young men being shipped to Germany as forced labor. (Marie-Dominique's father had been among them. He survived the trip, but died of tuberculosis contracted there.)

If Miaux had photographed these things or even recorded them in a diary, he would have risked imprisonment, even death, as a spy. But who would suspect an amateur poet? Poetry was like a cloak of invisibility, as the Allies knew. As D-Day approached, the British intelligence agency warned the French underground by broadcasting coded messages on the BBC. One text they used was Verlaine's "Chanson d'automne." The Germans listened to such transmissions as "Les sanglots longs / Des violons / De l'automne / Blessent mon coeur / D'une langueur / Monotone," thought, "Those crazy English. What are they on about now?" and shrugged it off.

Despite the urging from Berlin to hold out, the Germans in La Rochelle surrendered on May 7, 1945.

"You know," said the curator of the bunker, "we had that Doktor Jazz down here."

"Schultz-Köhn?" I said. "What was he doing in La Rochelle?"

"Something to do with the surrender. He didn't make a very good impression on the Americans, I hear."

"Why?"

"Apparently he asked if they had any Benny Goodman records."

One of the last of Miaux's poems celebrated the first harvest after liberation.

> *It's the month when the earth rejoices in its abundance*
> *When the hot sun brings the wheat to maturity*
> *When the stalks are heavy with grain*
> *And the harvesters gather them, singing.*

The poem was called "Messidor." Naturally.

46

THE PENDULUM PASSES

Les Halles, Paris 2me. October 1929. 2 a.m. 12°C.
As carts loaded with fruit and vegetables clop into the
lamplight, sleepy farm boys wake, stretch, and climb
down. Laborers off-load cauliflowers and potatoes and
haul them to wholesalers inside the glass-and-iron pa-
vilions. In Au Chien Qui Fume and other cafés, market
people slurp onion soup next to socialites in evening
dress who've stopped by to enjoy an early breakfast on
their way home from a party.

WE WHO LIVE IN PARIS ARE USED TO LIVING BY THE WEATHER
and the seasons. It's second nature now. We notice it the way we reg-
ister the clothes people wear. We may not comment on them, but it's
understood they are there to be noticed. Food also has a subliminal
language. To serve the new green asparagus or the *fraises des bois* in
the first week of their season conveys the host's culinary credentials
more succinctly than all the wine snobbery in the world.

Just as a scarf can be a fashion statement, depending on the
manner in which it's worn, the use of curtains or shutters in a room

and whether they are open or closed can signify a consciousness of atmosphere and all that goes with it. The novelist Françoise Sagan was a past mistress at such shades of meaning. The product of a wealthy family, she acquired this sense by osmosis. In her novel *La Chamade*, Lucile, the young mistress of wealthy businessman Charles, visits the home of Diane, an older woman rich enough to lead a life of leisure and self-gratification.

> Diane's apartment, in the Rue Cambon, looked very lovely, with fresh flowers everywhere, and even though the evening breeze was very mild and she had left the French doors open, big fires were burning in the two fireplaces, one at each end of the salon. Lucile, charmed by it all, moved about the room, alternately taking in whiffs of air from the street, already presaging the hot and dusty summer soon to come, and the smell of the flaming logs, which brought back for her the previous autumn, such a harsh one, inextricably linked in her memory with the woods in Sologne where Charles took her on hunts.
>
> "How elegant," said Lucile to Diane, "to have mixed two seasons in a single party."

With air-conditioning or central heating, such subtleties of the changing seasons would be lost. Rather, Parisians prefer to meet these seasonal variations head-on. Each change comes with losses and disappointments, promises and expectations, which they interpret according to their inclinations.

Food writer Ann Mah, for example, sees the seasons in terms of food. She writes,

> Fall has arrived in Paris. There is a northern wind in the air, and piles of crunchy leaves on the streets, and bushels of plums in the market to prove it. That quiche that I was making was for a picnic, one of the last of the season, and some friends and I enjoyed it on the Champ de Mars as we watched the golden late-summer day turn into a luminous evening lit by a blue moon and the sparkle of the Tour Eiffel.
>
> You'd think that I'd be sad, what with the disappearance of peaches and nectarines, and my imminent departure from Paris, and Paul Verlaine's gloomy refrain running through my head. But autumn has always been my favorite season, a time of new beginnings.

The art of living in France lies in adjusting to such new beginnings; even, as this writer does, relishing them for those variations of experience that make up the texture of the examined life—according to Socrates, the only one worth living.

Even before one opens one's eyes in the morning, one knows what season it is and where one is experiencing it. There is no mistaking, for example, a summer morning in Charente. Sand, carried from the beach only a few hundred meters from the door, sifts in through closed shutters and finds its way even into bed, so that one has to brush it off the sheets. Salt is always in the air. One tastes it on one's lips, feels it in a stickiness on the skin and the greasiness of ceramic basins and floor tiles. There can be few less inviting reminders that one is by the ocean than walking barefoot into the kitchen and stepping on a fat slug that has slithered in under the door from the garden.

In Paris, seasonal changes, particularly those of summer, are most evident in what happens in our own Parisian street. On our terrace, jasmine fills the night with its scent. The acacias come into leaf, shading the long windows that we leave open all night. Preparing dinner, I step out to clip fresh basil, parsley, mint, and thyme.

At the top of the street, tables and chairs are put out in front of the Théâtre de l'Odéon, turning the square into an outdoor café. At the same time, La Méditerranée restaurant, opposite the theater, opens its glass doors along the square, allowing its clientele to enjoy (or otherwise) the buskers performing "La Vie en rose" and the theme from *The Godfather*.

American novelist Irwin Shaw wrote about La Méditerranée and the theater in 1953:

You can look across the square to the Greek-styled theatre whose columns are illuminated each night by marvelously theatrical blue floodlights. Just after the Liberation, you could meet Jean Cocteau at that restaurant, and Christian

Bérard, bearded and carrying a tawny, long-furred cat. You could also get a fluffy chocolate mousse there, made with American Army chocolate, whose availability was no doubt connected with the nightly presence of the smiling, well-fed American soldier at the bar who must have been a mess sergeant.

Not much has changed in sixty-five years. Both the theater and restaurant are still there—the latter, however, without a bar and the former without floodlights, which offended its neighbors in what is now the most expensive district of Paris. Jean Cocteau and Christian Bérard are still present, Bérard in the mural he painted for one of La Méditerranée's dining rooms and Cocteau in the designs used on its marquee, linen, and china, based on a sketch he dashed off in its guest book. The American army has gone, but not the chocolate mousse, which still appears on the menu.

In many other cities, some of them even in France, La Méditerranée would long since have become a supermarket and the Théâtre de l'Odéon an ascetic performance complex in steel and glass, designed by a pupil of Jean Nouvel. That could still happen, but not, I like to think, on our watch.

POSTSCRIPT

THE FOOT OF OUR STREET, RUE DE L'ODÉON, CONVERGES WITH RUE de Condé, rue Monsieur-le-Prince, and boulevard Saint-Germain to create an open space, the Carrefour (crossroads) de l'Odéon. Bars and restaurants line the square, and just around the corner on the boulevard three cinema complexes attract long queues most afternoons and nights.

When I first moved to Paris, drivers—particularly on Saturday nights—would park around the square but also in the middle, leaving almost no space for traffic to pass. In summer, cars blocked the square and even edged onto the sidewalk as families abandoned them to stroll up to the Luxembourg Gardens. Occasional raids by the *pervenches* (periwinkles), as traffic policewomen were called because of their blue uniforms, didn't deter them. A few *papillons* (butterflies), slang for "traffic tickets," were regarded as part of the price of city living—and besides, in August no tickets were issued, since the *pervenches* were on holiday like almost everyone else.

Just when it seemed the city government was helpless to solve this problem, it intervened in a manner that was decisive, original, and entirely in tune with the traditions of Paris.

One Monday morning, a truck dumped slabs of stone in the middle of the square. Workers appeared, and by lunchtime they had dug up the cobblestones laid during Paris's reconstruction in the 1860s, exposed the subsoil, and created the beginnings of a traffic island. The next day they planted a tree, two or three meters tall and already in leaf.

By the end of the day, most of us had found a reason to walk down to the corner and stare at this addition to the neighborhood. A tree. Of course. Why hadn't we thought of that? Had it been just a traffic island, drivers would have found a way to park on it, but a tree . . . As nobody on our street was intimate with any plant larger than a geranium, we had to look it up. It was a paulownia, specifically the *Paulownia fortunei*, or dragon tree, which promised to blossom with purple flowers in the spring.

The following Saturday evening, some of us contrived to be relaxing with an aperitif outside the cafés on the carrefour. We took quiet satisfaction as driver after driver swung off the boulevard in expectation of parking in his customary spot, only to halt, glare up at the tree, and, muttering to himself, drive on.

Today the paulownia, now five or six meters tall, dominates the intersection, its purple blossoms a feature of the quartier. They have inspired the hotel opposite to decorate each of its windows with a box of geraniums and greatly increased trade at local cafés and restaurants, introducing an accent of rural calm to one's evening aperitif. During the publishers' annual trade show, the Salon du Livre, people hang books from its branches, and on the Fête de la

The Carrefour de l'Odéon, with paulownia tree.

Musique, when amateur musicians are encouraged to exercise their creativity in public, a children's choir performs under its shelter.

One Sunday evening shortly after I finished writing this book, Marie-Dominique came home from having dinner with her mother showing more good humor than was usual after these often trying occasions.

"I read something at *maman*'s place," she said, with the expression of the cat that has found the cream. "You know the carrefour?"

"Where they planted the tree?"

"Yes. Well, before they built the boulevard, that was the end of rue de l'Ancienne-Comédie. The cross street was called passage du Riche Laboureur, the Passage of the Rich Laborer."

"And so . . . ?"

"Guess who lived at 12 rue de l'Ancienne-Comédie?"

We'd discussed the theme of this book often enough for me to see what was coming.

"Let me guess. Fabre d'Églantine?"

"Yes!"

"Well, it makes sense," I mused, a little too unexcitedly. Marie-Dominique looked miffed, so I continued, "Danton lived just around the corner, and Desmoulins and Marat a few streets away. The Chapelle des Cordeliers is close too. But why the Rich Laborer?"

"It's from La Fontaine. One of his fables. Maybe there was an inn there that used the name."

Later, I looked up the story. Like most of La Fontaine's cautionary tales, the French equivalent of *Aesop's Fables*, it was in verse:

> *A wealthy farmer, feeling death draw nigh,*
> *Called round his children, and, no witness by,*
> *"Beware," he said, "of selling the estate*
> *Our fathers left us, purchased with their sweat;*
> *For hidden treasure's there.*
> *The spot I know not; but with zeal and care*
> *You'll find it out, and make it yours at last.*
> *Plough up the ground as soon as autumn's past,*
> *And dig and delve—nor grudge the daily pain;*

And when you've toiled, return and toil again."
He died. The sons turned up the field;
Incessant was their toil, and when the year
Was ended, large the produce it did yield,
Though ne'er a hidden treasure did appear.
Wise was the father, ere he died, to show
That labour is the mine whence riches flow.

It was almost too good to be true. For the author of the Republican calendar to live on a street that celebrated the rural virtues and to have the site of his former home marked by a tree—endings didn't come more fortuitous than that. And when the children gathered under its branches for the Fête de la Musique, what were the odds they sang "Il pleut, bergère"?

Life in France is less about achievement than process. Hours, days, months, seasons, years pass, each with promises honored or thwarted, events celebrated or endured. The world turns, but France, like the pivot of Foucault's pendulum, remains in its essentials unchanged. For such a culture the Republican calendar, preoccupied with nature and the seasons, may be, for all its faults, an apt metaphor and Philippe-François-Nazaire Fabre, however disreputable, a fitting laureate.

Important Dates and Events

JANUARY

1. Réveillon. The new year is welcomed in various locations, notably the Champs-Élyseés.

6. Nuit des Rois (Night of Kings). The traditional galette is shared.

10–13. The annual winter *soldes* (sales), at all stores.

17–21. Fashion Week: Men's.

21–25. Fashion Week: Haute Couture.

FEBRUARY

16–25. Chinese New Year. Parades in the thirteenth arrondissement.

27–March 6. Fashion Week Fall/Winter.

MARCH

Fashion Week Fall/Winter continues.

16–19. Salon du Livre, publishers' trade fair.

APRIL

Le Mois de la Photo (Month of Photography).

8. Paris Marathon.

11–14. Salon International du Livre Rare (rare book fair), Grand Palais.

MAY

19. Nuit des Musées (Night of Museums). Many Paris museums stay open late.

27–June 10. French Open tennis championship, Stade Roland-Garros.

JUNE

French Open continues.

21. Fête de la Musique. Amateur and professional musicians perform in public all night.

20–24. Fashion Week: Men's.

30. La Marche des Fiertés LGBT (LGBT pride march).

JULY

1–4. Fête du Cinéma. Reduced prices at participating cinemas.

1–5. Fashion Week: Haute Couture.

6. Paris Plages open (until September).

14. Bastille Day. France's national day, celebrated with a military parade down the Champs-Élysées and fireworks at night.

29. Climax of the Tour de France bicycle race. Final sprint down Champs-Élyseés.

AUGUST

Paris Plages remain open.

Outdoor film screenings at La Villette.

SEPTEMBER

8–16. Design Week.

16–17. Journées du Patrimoine. Open houses at various historic sites.

23–24. Fête des Jardins. Visits to private gardens.

OCTOBER

6. Nuit Blanche. Shops and cafés stay open all night. The mayor welcomes visitors to Hôtel de Ville.

11–14. *Vendange* of Montmartre vineyard. Montmartre Wine Festival.

19–22. FIAC (art fair for professional art dealers and gallerists), Grand Palais.

28–November 1. Salon du Chocolat.

NOVEMBER

15. Opening of the ski season at certain resorts.

DECEMBER

2. Opening of the ski season at certain resorts.

First weekend, through February or March. Ice skating at Hôtel de Ville and other venues.

ACKNOWLEDGMENTS

MY THANKS TO MY EDITOR, PETER HUBBARD, WHOSE IDEA THIS was; to Nick Amphlett, and to everyone at Harper Perennial who helped bring this book and many others to a successful completion. Also to my agent, Jonathan Lloyd of Curtis Brown; to my wife, Marie-Dominique, and daughter, Louise; to Neil Hornick for his reminiscences of busking around Europe, Ann Mah for permission to quote from her blog, and Janice Battiste, for her indispensable ability to retain her sanity and sense of humor when all about are losing theirs.

PHOTOGRAPHY AND ART CREDITS

GRAVURES, DOCUMENTS, AND ORIGINAL ART

Page v. Férat, M. *Paris sous la neige*. In *Le Monde illustré*, December 13, 1879.

Page 15. Unknown. *La Chaleur de Paris. Chapeaux pour chevaux*. In *Le Petit Parisien*.

Page 56. Groenia, Johannes. *L'Orage*. Author's collection.

Page 56. Veill, C. (engraver). *En Temps d'orage*. Author's collection.

Page 62. Anonymous. *Foucault's Pendulum in 1851*. Author's collection.

Page 74. Dien, P. (engraver). *Robespierre Squeezes Blood from Human Hearts*. Author's collection.

Page 79. Anonymous. *Georges Danton Making a Speech*. Author's collection.

Page 81. Thomire, Pierre Augustin. *Portrait of Fabre d'Églantine*. Museé des beaux-arts de Carcassonne.

Page 123. Gorguet, Auguste François. *A Melancholy Vision of April*. April 1892. Wikimedia Commons.

Page 131. Anonymous. *Portrait of Botanist André Thouin*. Author's collection.

Page 139. Guillaume, Albert. *En Canicule*. 1897. Author's collection.

Page 148. Daumier, Honoré. *Les Musiciens de Paris*. In *La Caricature*, November 11, 1874.

Page 156. Debucourt, Philibert-Louise. *The New Republic Rewrites the Calendar*. Author's collection.

Page 158. Lafitte, Louis. *Thermidor*. Author's collection.

Page 184. Cruikshank, George. *A Family Does a Moonlight Flit on Michaelmas*. Author's collection.

Page 189. Forest, Jean-Claude. *Barbarella and the Interstellar Florist*. In *Le Terrain Vague*, 1964.

Page 202. Cocteau, Jean. *Igor Stravinsky Composing* The Rite of Spring.

Page 221. Hemard, Joseph. *Brocante*. In *Le Grand Clapier de Paris*, editions de la Tournelle, 1946.

Page 239. Sager, Xavier. *Caricature of the Mistral*. 1905. Author's collection.

Page 240. Anonymous. *Des Vents; de la sphere*. Figure LXIII. Woodcut of storm with lightning. Author's collection.

Page 260. Lafitte, Louis. *Messidor*. Author's collection.

ORIGINAL DOCUMENTS.

Page 76. Original document dated Fructidor 8, Year 11. Author's collection.

Page 110. Khan, Yaseen. *Les Feuilles mortes*. Author's collection.

PHOTOGRAPHS

Page 17. Unknown. *Île de la Cité*. Service photo, Mairie de Paris.

Page 39. Unknown. *Marlene Dietrich in* Blonde Venus. 1933. Paramount-Publix Corporation.

Photography and Art Credits

Page 40. Unknown. *Umberto Eco. Paris Review.* Wikimedia Commons

Page 52. Montel, Marie-Dominique. *Author with Daughter.*

Page 138. Anonymous. *La Chaleur à Paris. Un marchand de Coco.* 1900s. Studio Meurisse.

Page 149. Hart, Bruce. *Neil Hornick and Sidewalkers in Copenhagen.*

Page 172. Anonymous. *Piscine Deligny.* June 1954. Author's collection.

Page 174. Anonymous. *Homework at Piscine Molitor.* August 1966. Agence France-Presse.

Page 175. Anonymous. *Micheline Bernardini at Piscine Molitor.* July 5, 1946. Author's collection.

Page 212. Anonymous. *François Mitterrand.* Archives AFP.

Page 232. Montel, Marie-Dominique. *Author with Musicians at Saint Jacques Festival.*

Page 243. *Hans Peter Litscher.* January 12, 2006. dpa picture alliance archive/Alamy Stock Photo.

Page 247. Anonymous. *Greta Garbo in Pajamas and Bare Feet.* 1928. Metro-Goldwyn-Mayer.

Page 255. Anonymous. *Jacques Chirac and Apples.* Service photo, Mairie de Paris.

Page 267. Bonneau, Francis. *Terrance Gelenter.*

PHOTOGRAPHS BY AUTHOR

Page xv. *Champs Élysées under Wheat,* 1990.

Page 29. *The Zouave* by Georges Diebolt on the Pont de l'Alma.

Page 33. *Le Téléphone* by Sophie Calle and Frank Gehry.

Page 51. *Alfred Dreyfus* statue by Louis Mittelberg.

Page 102. *La tempête et ses nuées* statue by Francois-Raoul Larche.

Page 111. *Yaseen Khan, Artist of the Paris Streets.*

Page 113. *Leaves at La Souris Verte.*

Page 290. *Carrefour de l'Odéon.*

INDEX

Page references in *italics* refer to illustrations.

About the Author

JOHN BAXTER has lived in Paris for almost thirty years. He is the author of many critically acclaimed books about France, including *Five Nights in Paris: After Dark in the City of Light*; *The Perfect Meal: In Search of the Lost Tastes of France* (winner of the International Association of Culinary Professionals Cookbook Award for Culinary Travel); *The Most Beautiful Walk in the World: A Pedestrian in Paris*; *Immoveable Feast: A Paris Christmas*, *Paris at the End of the World: The City of Light During the Great War, 1914–1918*; and *We'll Always Have Paris: Sex and Love in the City of Light*. Baxter, who gives literary walking tours through Paris, is also a film critic and biographer whose subjects have included the directors Federico Fellini, Stanley Kubrick, Woody Allen, and, most recently, Josef von Sternberg. Born in Australia, Baxter lives with his wife and daughter in the Saint-Germain-des-Prés neighborhood, in the building Sylvia Beach once called home.

For more information, visit www.johnbaxterparis.com.

ALSO BY JOHN BAXTER

THE MOST BEAUTIFUL WALK IN THE WORLD
A Pedestrian in Paris
A guided tour of the most beautiful walks through the City of Light.

MONTPARNASSE
Paris's District of Memory and Desire
In a ground-breaking reappraisal of this most glamorous of Paris's districts, Baxter looks beyond the nostalgia to the secret history of Montparnasse, a district where desire effaced memory and every taste could be satisfied—even those which were unexpressed.

MONTMARTRE
Paris's Village of Art and Sin
For visitors and armchair travelers alike, *Montmartre* captures the excitement and scandal of a fascinating quarter that condenses the elusive perfumes, colors and songs of Paris.

SAINT-GERMAIN-DES-PRÉS
Paris's Rebel Quarter
The award-winning chronicler of life in Paris reveals the secrets of his home quarter, Saint-Germain-des-Prés.

FIVE NIGHTS IN PARIS
After Dark in the City of Light
A feast for the mind and the senses, *Five Nights in Paris* takes you through the haunts of Paris's most storied artists and writers to the scenes of its most infamous crimes in a lively off-the-beaten-path tour not found in any guidebook.

PARIS AT THE END OF THE WORLD
The City of Light During the Great War, 1914-1918
John Baxter brilliantly brings to life one of the most dramatic and fascinating periods in the city's history.

THE PERFECT MEAL
In Search of the Lost Tastes of France
Part grand tour of France, part history of French cuisine, taking readers on a journey to discover and savor some of the world's great cultural achievements before they disappear completely.

IMMOVEABLE FEAST
A Paris Christmas
A warmhearted tale of good food, romance, family, and the Christmas spirit, Parisian style.

WE'LL ALWAYS HAVE PARIS
Sex and Love in the City of Light
A witty, audacious, scandalous behind-the-scenes excursion into the colorful all-night show that is Paris.

Available Wherever Books are Sold in Paperback and eBook